The Hidden Principalship

A Practical Handbook for New and Experienced Principals

Anthony Barber, EdD

ROWMAN & LITTLEFIELD EDUCATION
A division of
ROWMAN & LITTLEFIELD
Lanham • Boulder • New York • Toronto • Plymouth, UK

Published by Rowman & Littlefield Education
A division of Rowman & Littlefield
4501 Forbes Boulevard, Suite 200, Lanham, Maryland 20706
www.rowman.com

10 Thornbury Road, Plymouth PL6 7PP, United Kingdom

British Library Cataloguing in Publication Information Available

Library of Congress Cataloging-in-Publication Data

Library of Congress Cataloging-in-Publication Data Available

ISBN 978-1-4758-0560-4 (cloth : alk. paper)—ISBN 978-1-4758-0561-1 (pbk. : alk. paper)—ISBN 978-1-4758-0562-8 (electronic)

∞™ The paper used in this publication meets the minimum requirements of American National Standard for Information Sciences Permanence of Paper for Printed Library Materials, ANSI/NISO Z39.48-1992.

Printed in the United States of America

Contents

Disclaimer   v

Foreword   vii

Preface   ix

Acknowledgments   xi

1   Martial Arts Mentality   1

2   Try It: Making Change More Effective   5

3   The Meeting before the Meeting   11

4   How Many Is Many?   15

Quick Think   19

5   That's Why You Make the Big Bucks!   21

6   The "How Does That Work?" Meeting   25

Quick Think   29

7   Embrace the Antithesis   31

8   Common Threads: Investigating and Solving School Discipline   35

9   What's the Win?   39

10   You Don't Know What You Don't Know   43

Quick Think   47

11   The New Competition   49

12   The Fives Test   51

Quick Think   55

13   On Saving Face   57

14   Don't Bite the Boss   61

Quick Think   65

15   The "Buy In" Is Out!   67

16   Rock and Roll   71

17 My Miracle   75

Quick Think   77
18 They Have Forgotten Where They Are From   79
19 The Union with the Union   83

Quick Think   87
20 Too Much Good Can Be a Bad Thing   89
21 The Number Line of Change   93
22 Try It   97
23 Don't Try It   105
24 Case Studies   113

Situations   135
Conclusion   141
Bibliography   143
About the Author   145

Disclaimer

This text is offered solely as a guide and potential resource for educators who live and work in a constantly changing and dynamic environment. It is not intended to be and indeed is not an all-encompassing work that addresses each and every potential situation or issue that is or may be encountered in the realm of education. It does not provide a step-by-step guaranteed manual for success via wooden application of the concepts, ideas, and suggestions presented herein. Instead, this is a rendering and distillation of information crafted by an educator that may be of use to other educators. The application of that information is wholly dependent on the innumerable facts and circumstances and other intangible components that are part and parcel of each individual challenge or opportunity that may be presented in any individual situation.

Foreword

Are you tired of reading boring books on educational leadership? I know I am. Are you frustrated in learning about the "real" part of being a principal of a school, but you know the information contained in many principal books doesn't tell the entire story? I know I am. Well, I have some good news for you.

The Hidden Principalship
A Practical Handbook for New and Experienced Principals
by Dr. Anthony Barber

It will not let you down.

This is the book you need to keep on your nightstand when you need help. If I had just one book to read about being a principal, this is it. Each of the twenty-four chapters is loaded with practical ideas and insightful information. I only wish I had read this book when I first became a principal. Everyone needs advice. Everyone is looking for a silver bullet. We all know there is no such thing. However, Anthony Barber's *The Hidden Principalship* is as close as it gets. You should probably buy a second copy and give it to your top "teacher-leader."

Dr. James P. Capolupo
Superintendent, Springfield School District
National Superintendent of the Year Finalist

Preface

You are a principal. Or you are in a principal program. Or you are thinking about a principal program. Or maybe you just liked the cover of this book and thought, *Let me check it out*. Whatever the reason, let us assume you have some interest in the real juice about the principalship. You know, the nitty-gritty, down and dirty stuff that most professors either don't know or fail to share, as this information could discourage you from sending that next tuition payment.

Admittedly, this text is not for the faint of heart; however, the intent is not to deter you from becoming a principal. On the contrary, we wish for you to be the best principal your school has ever seen! But to be the best, one has to ascertain knowledge. Lots of it! And this script has plenty to share.

In studying the available principal-education texts, there was no need for another book about using data or involving the stakeholders in the decision-making process. And we certainly have plenty of "feel good" stories about leadership, teamwork, CIAs, PLCs, ABCs, et cetera, et cetera, and et cetera. Get my drift? These topics are all critically important to the success of any administrator, but much like my Aunt Gert's Thanksgiving Day turkey, quite overdone. (*Sorry Aunt Gert.*)

Safe to say, the principal professional library lacks a "tell it all" text to assist us in seeing what the naked eye cannot about the principalship. For example, do you own a house? Did you have a home inspection? Chances are, you probably did. In some cases, the inspection may have put the brakes on the sale; perhaps in others, it did not. For my family, the inspection gave us peace of mind by having an expert examine all of the items we could not.

For instance, as we were admiring the color schemes and counter space, our inspector was checking for Radon, foundation cracks, and HVAC issues. Thankfully, none of the major home issues presented as problems, and we were able to purchase the house. However, wouldn't you know the counter had a crack in it and had to be replaced? Figures!

Needless to say, becoming a principal is similar to purchasing a house. It is an investment. A *huge* investment! Consider this book your "inspection" of the principalship. *As others are admiring the paint colors, this text examines the foundation.* We are going to review issues of power, change, and culture, but in a way that differs from the traditional ways that these and other topics may have been previously presented to you.

Our job is to expose the cracks in the foundation so you can *see* them and *decide* how you will handle them (and at a lower price than any home inspection would ever cost).

Chapters are written as short vignettes: some anecdotal, others straightforward. And each chapter will provide a "Practical Advice" section. Feel free to skip around to the chapters that interest you or just read front to back, back to front, or however you choose.

Please note that these ideas are ever-present and always around us. As you are reading, you might say to yourself (or even out loud), "Duh. I knew that." If you should have a "Duh" moment, that's awesome! The key is to continue to recall these and other points as you enter into this profession.

It is one thing to know the plays during practice and quite another to execute those plays while in the game. That's what separates the contenders from the pretenders. Keeping this information in the forefront of your playbook will assist you on your way to a championship year.

Thank you for purchasing this text. We do appreciate it and anticipate many successes for your future. Whether you become a principal or not, hopefully you will glean (love that word) a more in-depth understanding of the "off-the-record" culture that exists within this and every job.

As Pip would say in *Great Expectations*, I wish you "well and happy."

Acknowledgments

To my wife, Denise, and my sons, Brett, Braden, and Bradley, you are the reason! Thank you for always being and believing. I will always love you.

Mom and Dad! These are the heroes of my life. My parents, who struggled so hard so that my brothers and I could become educated, are my cornerstones.

My brothers, Mike and Bill, have inspired me more than they will ever know. Both, through their commitment to their hopes, their dreams, and their families, have shown me what it means to be successful and happy.

Mr. Jeffrey Ulmer has been a true inspiration to me professionally and personally. Thanks for being my partner and my best friend.

Dr. Edward Rozycki has been a constant in my quest for higher knowledge. His encouragement and intellectual insight as both my professor and my advisor have inspired me to always "think beyond the first decision."

I would like to thank Wilson, my silent friend, who speaks to me when no one else is around. There are times in life when we need a little guidance from ourselves. It just seems more possible coming from a volleyball.

ONE

Martial Arts Mentality

Sensei Jason Felix is a martial arts instructor, and someone who is respected and admired. In fact, he is quite an amazing person. From modest beginnings, Sensei Felix graduated from a distinguished university, went to law school, earned his law degree, is a practicing lawyer, and has a lovely wife, three great sons, and a tremendously successful karate business. Yet, of all the titles that Sensei Jason Felix holds, the one that has had the most profound impact is the one you would least expect.

While attending a social function, a father once shared a powerful story about Sensei Felix:

> I have two sons, and my oldest son wanted to take karate. Not knowing much about it, I did a little research and found out that there was a tremendous karate school right in our backyard. My son, Joel, and I ventured out one fine Saturday morning to the dojo. I must admit, after reading and hearing so much about Sensei Felix, I was feeling a bit nervous. We have all seen Karate Kid movies, and quite frankly, when someone has attained the level of sensei, my assumption was that this dude was going to be unapproachable.
>
> As Joel and I had entered the dojo, a man came up to me and said, "Hello there. Welcome to the dojo." As he shook my hand, he knelt down to see Joel eye to eye, slapped him five, and said, "Hi buddy. I'm glad you are here. I'm Jason. What's your name?"
>
> No sensei entrance. No "Council Jason Felix at your service" greeting. No kissing the ring or lighting a ceremony candle. None of that rubbish! "I'm Jason." Just Jason.

Needless to say, the impression was made!

Now the skeptics of the world may not believe this story or may think that this is a good way to drum up business—be nice going in, make sure the check cashes, and then it's *hammer time*. (You are welcome, MC.) Likewise, it would have been darn easy for Jason to start with the title of sensei or council. He did the time; he had the degrees. Many would think he had earned that right. In theory, he had.

But martial art is different in that respect. The practice of karate is one of self-defense. Its purpose is to learn the discipline and movements so that one never has to use them. (Quite different from the days of Ralph Macchio.) Imagine spending countless hours, days, and even years to learn something in the hopes of never having to use it! *So true is the discipline of earning status with humility.*

So often, people aspire and attain such lofty heights only to fall back on the insecurities that exist within us. And for what—to puff our chests out over some accolade or impress our neighbor with our latest accomplishment? Nonsense! When you are the principal, everyone knows who you are. We need not remind people every time the chance presents itself. So knock that stuff off.

It is not good when someone attains the level of the principal only to act like a "tough guy" with the sole purpose of thwarting those who have stepped on him along the way. It is like folks who were bullied on the playground grew up, became principals, and are now going to make their retribution felt. Please! To be the man, you don't have to beat the man. You just have to be.

Use the golden rule, and use it with unbridled passion. Look for ways to downplay your accomplishments and highlight others. Just as we desire the focus to be on the students and not the teachers in the classroom, so too the focus of the school should be on the people and not the boss.

One of my smartest friends, Gloria, once said, "There is a difference between saying you are a great principal, and quite another by shutting your mouth and proving it." I could not have said it any better! If Sensei Jason Felix can start with just Jason, consider the possibilities for us.

So true is the discipline of earning status with humility.

PRACTICAL ADVICE

What type of car do you drive? Did you run out and buy the latest fancy-pants car when you got the job? Hold on now. Be smart. What message would that send to your colleagues? I am not saying that driving a luxury automobile is malevolent, but consider the indirect message you will be sending to the staff: "I'm more important than you." Remember what happen to the guy in Goodfellas who went out and bought the new car? All good things in time.

Karate is for self-defense only. If you should happen to earn your doctorate degree or attain another accolade, present with modesty. Look for ways to share the limelight. Earn the degrees, attain your letters, and then place them behind your name and leave them there. Like karate, use them only when necessary: resumes, business cards, and so forth. Remember, we all know who the principal is!

Do you have a principal's parking spot? Do you really need it? I know. I know. You get called to central office and other meetings that require you to be out of the building, and it is nice to have a spot when returning, especially when it's raining. However, recall *The Servant Leader*. The principal's spot is a symbol of status. And one that is unnecessary. If you really want to make a hit with the staff, make it a teacher-of-the-week spot, and then make darn sure everyone will have a turn.

Be wary of possessive pronouns. If another principal refers to the assistant principal as "my assistant," I am going to freak out! They are not your assistants! They are the assistants for the school. And in fact, the term *assistant* is a tad disrespectful. They are principals. They have different tasks, but all in all, they are principals.

There once was a boss who had a thing for calling his assistants his *"Ass"*-istants. Needless to say, they didn't find that amusing. It's not "your" school, "your" staff, or "your" students. They are ours, all of ours. Look for opportunities to not only present a team approach, but also live it.

TWO

Try It

Making Change More Effective

Remember that cute 1970s commercial for Life cereal with little Mikey? His brothers were resistant to trying the new cereal, which was "supposed to be good for you." Being clever, as siblings can be, they passed the bowl to their little brother, Mikey. As fate would have it, Mikey tried it, and Mikey liked it! "Nutritious and delicious." What a concept!

Now whether or not you can recall this curt but effective ad, hopefully the concept resonates—taste tests work! Recently, I attended a colleague's faculty meeting. He was presenting useful reading strategies to his staff (or so that is what he said). Once in the meeting, the lights dimmed, the PowerPoint brightened, and the principal began to talk . . . and talk . . . and talk.

Instead of sharing the reading strategies with his staff (or better yet, tagging a staff member to be the expert), he presented the research. Tons of it! The entire premise was a call for "every teacher to be a reading teacher," and his mission was to convince his staff of this "moral imperative." A valuable tenet, but the weary looks told the story—the staff had checked out.

Have you ever attended a meeting like this? Or worse, have you ever been the presenter?

When educators can step out of the educational world, we can learn so much. For example, have you ever been to a supermarket and had someone offer you a stick of cheese? Free samples! Sometimes it tastes good; other times not, but the risk-to-reward factor makes it prosperous. Free works, especially with a new product.

Now, picture the cheese lady, instead of offering cheese, dispensing volumes of literature about cheese. Facts about how their product is so much better. Four out of five doctors recommend it. Blah. Blah. Blah. As the consumer, you are less likely to stop for literature because the risk-to-reward factor is low. "I am not here to read. I am here to eat!"

How does this short vignette relate to us as educational leaders? When we start with the research, we sometimes become the cheese lady without cheese. Have you ever heard a teacher say, "Just tell me what you want me to do?" And yet as "instructional leaders," we tend to view these simple requests as antagonistic or detached. We outfox ourselves by demonstrating our expertise through degrees of documentation. We wallpaper our hallways with slogans of "every teacher is a reading teacher," only to create the same eye-rolling reaction that you would give to the cheese lady with her informational handouts.

Culture, by definition, depicts the way we do what we do in a society.[1] Culture exists on three levels: technical, formal, and informal.[2] On the technical level, people do things because they *work*. For example, when starting a car, we put the key into the ignition gauge not for fun, but because we want the car to start. Key in, engine on. It works!

On the formal level, people do things because they are *right* for them. An example of formal culture is that habitual jaunt to Starbucks every Friday. We chose this pattern because it is right for us. Formal culture requires negotiation because it is "tied to feelings and resistant to change."[3] In other words, trying to break the pattern of your venti vanilla cappuccino may not be as easy as we think . . . especially if it is made with soy and a smidgen of whipped cream. Delightful!

The informal culture is nonexistent to us until the formal culture is broken by a change. For instance, imagine the first person to wear his baseball cap to the side. That is informal culture, representing a "shock" to the formal system. Informal culture becomes formal when people start to acknowledge the change. As others start to wear their hats to the side, the actions become accepted—a change in accepted behavior.

Educational experts foil their own expertise by relying too much on the anticipated argument (formal) and far to less on the attainable action (technical).

Please note, sound research and data analysis should precipitate and continue to support change. Perform the research first, select a few workable ideas that you want to try, and then let the staff test them in a nonthreatening environment.

Even the greatest research in the world has to take context into account, meaning just because it "was right" for one school, that does not mean it can transfer to another seamlessly. Forcing one way for people to "do something" brings with it the idea that this is the correct way. In being correct, all others must be incorrect. When we allow our teachers the chance to try and experiment, we allow culture to do what it does . . . guide us on ways to function within the given society.

Skillful leaders set the stage by offering the professionals a chance to be just that—professional. For instance, instead of my friend's faculty meeting, imagine if this correspondence were emailed to the staff:

> Good morning everyone. Our data team is noticing some negative trends in our data when it comes to making inferences. For our next department meeting, can we work together to brainstorm some of the ways that you handle this in your classroom? If we can all bring one or two strategies with you to share, that would be terrific. And if you do not have one, no worries. That's why we are a team. See you all at 3:00 p.m. I'll bring the pretzels.

Quite a different approach than starting with the assumption that no one knows what they are doing. Now, if you do get to the meeting and see the ideas are limited, then bring in the cavalry. However, my gut feeling is that someone will "have it" and be willing to share. As the discourse commences, the strategies become a focal point for teamwork and cooperation.

Perhaps you can ask a few people to model it in their classrooms. Try it out; see if it works, and report back to the staff on the next meeting day. Perhaps the ones that work will be copied and repeated by others. Don't look now, but every teacher is starting to become a teacher of reading.

Teachers are like independent contractors. This does not mean to say these people are not team oriented or collaborative. Indeed, there are fantastic teams that plan together and are consistent in their approach to curriculum, instruction, and assessment. However, our teams are not working with widgets; different students present different challenges and opportunities.

We have to have the forethought to plan before crisis occurs by allowing our teachers the chance to test actions prior to believing lock, stock, and barrel. In a sense, you are not putting the cart in front of the horse, only allowing the consumer a chance to sample what is in the cart prior to setting it in motion.

This theory works best when teams are not in crisis. For those moments, a leader may have to make a command decision. In non-crisis situations, we have the benefit of time, which allows us to "try" different approaches. To stay with our analogy, if one needs to pick up napkins for a party for which you are extremely late, you may not have time to try the cheese. The taste test works best with shoppers (nonspecific time frame) rather than buyers (specific, targeted time frame).

Research is used to "win" arguments. If someone is starting with research, perhaps the hidden message to the listener is one of anticipated disagreement. It seems so easy, but then so is handing out free cheese, and yet, there lies the brilliance of the innovation.

To transform culture, change has to be good for the individual as well as the organization.

Formal culture is negotiated, meaning that sustained society changes occur when the majority of people deem the action to be worth sustaining. To do this well, we as educational leaders must be open to disagreement and variation. We must embrace the antithesis of our beliefs as long as the desired outcomes are reached for the good of all.

Perhaps Mikey's brothers would have made exceptional administrators. Perhaps there is a little bit of Mikey in all of us. By allowing our teachers to grab their spoons and dig into different approaches, different ideas, we build professional development that is founded on choice, motivation, and what works!

In your next professional-development session, try using make-and-takes, share-fests, and conference-like setups, where differentiation is the norm. Allow the *grassroots* (culture) to cultivate the change process by trusting your staff to use what works for them. "Nutritious and delicious!" *Bon appetit!*

PRACTICAL ADVICE

Have a school advisory team. School advisory teams are a great way to have folks come together and plan for the needs of the school. Use these as data meetings or other types of informative sessions where the team reviews the goals of the district and school and looks to maximize their ability to reach them. Also, professional-development planning can be part of this team's focus. Remember, you don't know everything. Utilize the power of the team. Be sure to make the team voluntary.

The resident expert lives on campus. Most times, people who own consulting firms were once teachers. They had an idea and took a chance on starting the company with the hopes of securing a certain outcome (more money, more free time, etc.). However, this does not mean that the people in your building are less innovative or less intelligent when it comes to all sorts of ideas for teaching and learning.

Before you run out and book the next guru to appear at your in-service, check with your staff first. Use the research/data team to identify items of need and then plan with your people. If you have to use an expert, have someone trained, and then have that person present to the staff. Remember, the staff wants to teach. Give the people what they want!

Use conference-style in-service. The best part about a conference (besides seeing friends and making new ones) is the ability to program for your interests/needs. Conferences are a great way to differentiate to the masses by providing choice. Use this style of in-service whenever possible with your staff. Be sure to ask different people to be presenters at different times. Practice differentiation.

NOTES

1. K. G. Clabaugh and G. E. Rozycki, *Understanding Schools: The Foundations of Education* (New York: Harper & Row, 1990).

2. Edward T. Hall, *The Silent Language* (Greenwich, CT: Fawcett, 1959).

3. Clabaugh and Rozycki, *Understanding Schools*.

THREE

The Meeting before the Meeting

Things do not get done at the meeting; they get done at the meetings before the meeting. Period! The sooner you learn this practice, the easier life will be for you as a principal.

More often than not, meetings occur because some sort of outcome is being solicited. Be it discipline hearings, curriculum writing sessions, committee work, whatever. People gather for various reasons, yet the single factor that threads all of these events is the outcome. Most times, we are not gathering just for the sake of meeting, although we have all been at plenty of those "summits" too.

The reason that meetings become derailed or just chatter sessions is because of the dynamics of culture and trust. Aside from a significant birthday, proposal, or pregnancy, surprises are not always good. For example, do you cringe when the car mechanic calls? You know, drop the car off for a quick oil change and . . . surprise—you need brakes! I usually retort with a comment like, "Really, brakes? Are you sure?"

Inevitably, the mechanic gives the Oscar-winning performance about how unsafe the car is and how he wouldn't drive his own family in the car in the current condition. After a few minutes of his melodramatic soliloquy, I start to hear the sound of my credit card swiping through the pin pad. Lovely.

Hopefully, you trust your mechanic, so aside from the occasional recitals, you believe what he is saying. But what if you did not? What if you had doubts? Doubts about the car? Doubts about his integrity? See where this is going? Sometimes people go into meetings with one idea (oil change) and end up "hearing" so much more (brakes, tires, flux capacitor, etc.), even if it is not intended. Why? *Because without having the opportunity to digest information, we create mistrust.*

Think about the end of car commercials and that ridiculous legal jumbo that someone spits out like a sneeze gone wrong—"tax and tags not included, 4.5 percent increase at time of signing, first born subject to late payments and so on, and so on." Think about the way the volume gets lower and the speed increases from the rest of the commercial. Very strategic, but perhaps the speed of the delivery creates suspicion. Perhaps the lower volume creates concern. (Perhaps I use *perhaps* too much? Perhaps.)

People relate information through individual means—personal impact. Our brains question new ideas by putting up defenses to them. Be it time, too much information, disagreement, and so on, some people tend to get defensive to new ideas at first. Call it playing devil's advocate.

Some use Maslow's Hierarchy of Needs in meetings when dealing with new initiatives. They ask presenters to go through the process starting with the physiological needs: food, water, shelter. In a sense, they try to "block" new ideas if the person has not thought out the basic procedural impacts.

If you truly desire a certain outcome from a meeting, take the time to set the stage with the players.

For instance, if you are going into a major staffing meeting and know what internal and external moves are going to be discussed, do not wait until that day to share your plans. (There have been plenty of situations where a principal has played possum at staffing meetings. We might "win today" with a certain move or block, but lose the next time by creating a feeling of mistrust among our colleagues.)

We are better off meeting with players separately or in small groups. Find out what they need/want. Do less talking and more listening (remember the car commercial). Maybe you will find a huge support for your ideas, or maybe you will find out people think your ideas are awful. Either way, you win by not assuming and providing opportunities to dialogue.

We all need time to process. Be sure to build it into your next think-tank session.

PRACTICAL ADVICE

Get to know the people who cannot keep their mouth shut. This may seem callous, but it is a very useful way to get out information to the masses without actually having a meeting. A friend of mine told me about an instance when he was really upset about a homework guideline that was being created by one of his action teams. So one morning he happened to "share" that information to a certain person, and no lie, by day's end, the guideline was changed. No meeting. No mess.

Obviously, you would never share personal information about anyone or any situation, but for these less significant issues, a little whisper down the lane does work on occasion. Now, if you don't want people to know something, remember this person.

If the decision is already made, then just say it. Nothing irritates busy people more than having to attend a meeting where everyone knows the decision has already been made, but is being presented as open to debate. As the principal, you are allowed to make decisions. You are allowed to say, "This is the way it is going to be." Now, one should not make that a habit, and certainly you are better off making those command decisions in crisis rather than peace. However, you do possess that right. Like karate, use when no other options exist.

Don't write a check your rear end can't cash. How many times do we see people get into bad situations when they promise something that cannot possibly happen? For instance, there was a principal who promised the student body a field trip to an amusement park for high performance on a state standardized test. Well, the students held up their part of the bargain, but when it came time to collect, the principal had forgotten to first check the board policies. She had no meetings with anyone prior to mentioning it one day on school television. Needless to say, the trip was not approved. Not good. Not good at all.

FOUR

How Many Is Many?

Martha, a principal in a suburban middle school, was not having a good day. Earlier, Doug, one of her team leaders, told her that the staff members were commenting about her indecisiveness. In short, there was an issue brewing over whether or not to change the two-hour delay schedule. Lost prep times, coverage, you get the picture. In wanting to be thorough, Martha was going through the protocol and checking in with the various stakeholders—that is, having the meetings before the meeting. (Good job, Martha!)

Doug, the team leader, was a good-hearted individual. He had always wanted what was best for the school and never demonstrated any ill will toward Martha. In trusting Doug's character, Martha assumed truth in his statement. Steadily, her feelings went from apprehension to anger. "Indecisive?" She thought to herself. "Here I am trying to make sure we are doing the right thing, and they think I am being indecisive."

In no more than ten minutes, Martha had scheduled an after-school faculty meeting. And as fate would have it, Martha's day went from bad to worse. For although no one spoke at the faculty meeting except Martha, the silence from her audience was loud and clear.

Should Martha have scheduled a faculty meeting? Should she have met with the team leaders? Sent an email? What would you have done?

Our sensitive nature is often what makes us so compassionate toward our students and staff, but it can also be a source of self-doubt. As teachers, kids talk about us all the time. Some good, some bad. The difference is we are not hanging out with them on a Friday night when the conversations are happening; therefore, that type of "in your face" criticism is not present on a daily basis. This is not the case for the principal.

As the principal, you should expect the criticism. Much like a coach of a professional football team, the buck stops with you, and there are a myriad of Monday-morning quarterbacks waiting to question your decisions. To be a principal, you need thick skin, *really thick*! You are going to be questioned; people will sometimes not like your decisions. That's okay, and in fact, it's a good thing.

Our job is sometimes delegating limited resources to people in our environment. Therefore, having people upset with you based on these decisions is not only expected, but also necessary to keep the balance of these special-interest groups. Call it triage in the school system. *Everything cannot be a priority.* As the leader, you and your team will have to make those decisions and set precedence to them.

In this particular scenario, Martha overestimated the "many." Upon hearing criticisms, ideas, explanations, we must realize that there is strength in *perceived* numbers. Come on, do you really think that the entire staff feels the same way on a given issue? Don't you think that if things were that bad, there would be other signs—more people coming to you, district office involvement, parental calls, emails, and so forth? Get the picture?

Assuming that "everyone" is involved is ill advised. Do your homework to quantify the numbers; remember the meetings before the meeting. Check to see what people are thinking before you react. Remember, we can think anything, but once we say it, we own it. Are you sure you want to go in front of the staff with this issue? If you hesitate trying to answer this question, don't do it.

And what of our friend, Doug? Doug heard this information and decided to report it to Martha. Why? True, he could have had genuine concern for her reputation. Or perhaps he was clearing his. Think about it. He just heard it today. This was his prep period. He had been teaching all day, had lunch, and was now on his prep period. Did he really have time to speak to the staff, the "whole" staff? Nope. Not a chance.

Can we deduce from this scenario that Martha probably was getting roasted at lunch and Doug felt bad? Maybe. Maybe not. But the situation certainly did not call for an all-out assault on the entire staff. And if Martha thinks that is the last time she will be talked about in a negative fashion at lunch, think again. Take the job, and our ears are going to burn from here to Timbuktu. That's just the nature of the beast.

PRACTICAL ADVICE

Reread the meeting-before-the-meeting chapter. Do the research. Calculate the information, and then decide whether to react or not. We do not succeed in situations by rushing into them in an emotional state. We succeed by using our intellects. We succeed by following a protocol and trusting the process to get there.

If you are scared, get a dog—but don't become a principal. If you truly are the type of person that has stomach issues every time someone is mad at you, please do us all a favor, and think about another career move. We are not saying that you want to be a jerk in this job. On the contrary, you want to be compassionate, understanding, and genuine to all. But think about it—if you are really doing your job well, you may have to rate someone unsatisfactory, fire a substitute teacher, call Children and Youth on a family, and talk to the police for a bullying situation all before lunch! Think you are going to break a few eggs with that order?

Remember Oedipus. The story of Oedipus demonstrates the point that sometimes it is better to leave well enough alone. Maybe it is time to sit the "Dougs" of the school down and let them know that although you appreciate their concern, you really do not want to get involved in the gossip game. As stated previously, people will chatter. Perhaps it is best to know when it is serious rather than just the latest news. Let sleeping Dougs lie.

On being the boss. Did you ever poke fun at your boss? Then don't be surprised that it is coming back to you. That's just the circumstance of leadership. *Each time you ascend a rung on the leadership ladder, note that your rear end is showing a little extra and to more people.* Thick skin, my friend. Thick skin.

Quick Think

The role of leadership is not to make everyone happy. People will be happy when the conditions for success are attainable and the measures are defined.

FIVE

That's Why You Make the Big Bucks!

Mr. Flesher stood in the front lobby when the students from Jacksonville Middle School arrived. Although he was not required to be there, he wanted to make sure he did his part to start each child's day off with a high five and a smile.

On one particular day, the principal, Dr. Janice West, was rushing out to one of the buses. A bit frazzled, she darted passed Mr. Flesher without even saying a word. About ten minutes later, Dr. West finally came back into the building. Seeing Mr. Flesher still there, she stated, "It's going to be one of those days," as she rushed by him to go attend to her next "principal" task.

Mr. Flesher, in a pleasant of voice, stated, "I guess that's why you make the big bucks."

Dr. West replied, "I guess so," as she vanished into her office. Almost instantaneously, the bell rang, and Mr. Flesher slowly made his way to homeroom.

As one can imagine, this scene plays out in a similar fashion across our country and beyond. Today's schools are in constant motion, and the daily duties that each of us attend to seem almost as infinite as pi. However, despite the fact that sometimes it can be "one of those days," the exchange between Mr. Flesher and Dr. West is also fairly common and often the root of hidden issues within the dynamics of school culture.

Did you ever notice how often teachers and administrators communicate, but fail to actually talk with one another?

It is almost comical to watch—highly intelligent human beings engaging in "exhilarating" discussions only to completely forget what was said the moment the conversation ends. The entire practice brings me back to my high school days and Mr. Burg's social studies class. He'd talk; we'd listen. Tests were on Fridays, and rest assured, by Saturday morning, my brain was completely devoid of anything from the previous day.

21

Unfortunately, we have all experienced a Mr. Burg class. As I think through those courses, it becomes apparent how much he talked, but again how little was corresponded. Mr. Burg failed to make a *connection* with our class. Like the relationship between Mr. Flesher and Dr. West, the surface sufficed, and any extension into a more robust relationship was politely dismissed.

Why do teachers use clichés toward administers? What are they trying to tell us? Are we listening? Why do we allow the cliché to end thought when it should just begin it?

Clichés often present a dismissive significance toward the topic. Call it a polite indifference or civil compliance until safer confines are found. Maybe "that's why you make the big bucks" tells the administrator she is alone—informing her that this person does not feel confident in the relationship to speak the truth.

Remember, formal culture is negotiated between the individuals and represents their acceptance on "how things get done."

The interactions we employ as human beings are created and reinforced by our agreement or non-agreement. In other words, we are actually *agreeing* to not communicate by accepting the surface talk or easily dismissed jargon. It is within the approval of this cultural norm that we diminish our ability to be fully functional as a team.

When a teacher uses a cliché, it is the administrator's responsibility to solicit further information. We cannot allow the cliché to end our conversations. As administrators, we must work in earnest to provide opportunities for honest, two-way feedback. Surveys, committees, and think-tanks are all great ways to approach the real conversations. However, the greatest tool we have is the one-on-one personal conversation that so often is devoid in busy environments.

Another timeless cliché is "they have forgotten where they are from." Referenced by teachers toward administrators, this cliché best embodies the possible glimpse into the understanding of our staff. If teachers truly believe we (as administrators) have lost touch with the practice of understanding their situation/reality, then we have successfully created a counterculture to the essential mission—producing an environment conducive for learning *for all*. Culture is felt from the moment one steps into a school. Without having the appropriate supports, we create the king's new clothes.

The foundation for a solid relationship resides in our commitment to develop it. Our ability to recognize the genuine value of nurturing a relationship will ultimately lead to its flourishing.

PRACTICAL ADVICE

Make the time. We are all very busy people. But that is not an excuse to dismiss the human spirit and our need for connection. We must recognize the "critical moments" of our profession. We must strive to make each person feel connected and appreciated for who they are. Make time to talk to people. Get to know them personally and professionally. If you care, they will as well.

Solicit input. The only way to build the trust for input is to value it. People that ask for others' ideas only to use their own eventually lose the genuine spirit of teamwork. Involve as many as you can when you can.

Challenge the cliché in the nicest of ways. Maybe not during the moment, but afterward, go to the person and ask politely what she was trying to tell you. Assure her that you are not being accusatory, only that you are looking to be a better principal and person.

Explain your reasoning behind decisions. If you make a critical decision, explain your process. Do not assume everyone knows the dynamics and background. People might not always agree with your decisions, but you will gain the respect of your peers by making the time to answer questions. You may not "owe" them a reason, but. . . .

SIX

The "How Does That Work?" Meeting

Did you ever have to defend your teaching job to non-educators? You know, you go out to dinner with some friends, order a few appetizers, and no sooner the Calamari comes, the chatter starts. "You only work nine months. You get prep periods. How tough can it be?" Trying to keep your composure, you do your best to explain the amount of work that goes into preparing for a lesson. From the planning and production to the gathering and grading, minutes turn to hours, as you recall gazing at the clock on Sunday nights to see the 9:00 p.m. turn to 11:00 p.m. and think, *Where did my weekend go?* Remember those days?

Try as we may, many times our justifications fall on deaf ears. Now, do not believe that your dinner guests were ill-natured in their comments. (They were supposed to be friends.) However, the comments do hint at suspicion. Assume it is just hard to comprehend. People who hang drywall for a living can perceive their finished product. But folks cannot always "see" what teachers do! Never holding the job, the assumptions get the better of people and turn into conspiracies. "Would you look at the time. Check, please."

As teachers, it is difficult to have outside people visit our classrooms. People have jobs, and even though they may be *interested* at dinner, the stake of giving up a day's pay to learn about our job is improbable. (Here is where the principal has a distinct advantage over the teacher.)

For the principal, the captive audience is with us. Think about it; the teachers are there every day. And just as your friends may question aspects of your job, the assumption that teachers are questioning yours is a sure bet. ("What do they do up there all day?") With that being stated, it is our responsibility to "educate" our staff about aspects of the school (and our job) that attract considerable attention at the faculty-room lunch table, but not so much at public meetings.

As a teacher, did you ever wonder how supplement contracts were selected? Or how teachers are chosen between level-1 or level-2 classes? Or how discipline was processed? So if you had those thoughts. . . . See where this is going?

Just because we are not necessarily "in the classroom" does not mean we should stop teaching. In fact, it is imperative that we continue to educate folks, especially the inquiring minds of our school. Here is where the "How does that work?" format functions so well.

Instead of having a typical faculty meeting (yawn), let the staff know that you are going to be covering two "How does that work?" topics. Order some refreshments and have a go at it. If you cannot afford to "surrender" a meeting, hold an optional session before or after school. Make the meeting voluntary. This way, you have a captive audience. I have even seen a principal hold "lunch bunch" sessions, where she bought lunch for the people who came to the mini-meeting. A couple pizzas and a plan! Pretty cool!

In addition, you do not have to know everything. Survey your staff for topics or possible things they might like to share with their colleagues. They will let you know what is on their mind. This is a great way to address the informal culture that can undermine morale. By establishing the dialogue, we open the communication pathways to discuss a host of possibilities.

One of the greatest resources we have to break cultural divide is sharing our experiences. Use them or lose them!

PRACTICAL ADVICE

Start with a win. Be sure that the first time you attempt to have a session you start with a topic that you know well, but don't stack the deck. On the contrary, these sessions are great for honest dialogue and learning from both ends—teacher and principal. However, for the inaugural one, pick a topic that is not too controversial.

Survey the staff. As mentioned previously, be sure to survey the staff on topics of interest. As the sessions start to commence, do not be surprised if the topics get more intense. When this occurs, smile. The more comfortable the staff feels about mentioning a tough topic, the more you are penetrating the informal culture. Stay calm. Do not take personal offense.

Remember your friends at dinner. They are still your friends. Give them the knowledge to help them formulate a different interpretation. If they do, great. If they do not, great. Either way, you have done what you needed to do. Nice work.

Allow the staff to present. There may be topics that need to be explained to the staff that are generated from them as well. In those instances, be supportive and allow the process to function. Remember, any time you don't give the big speech, you win! Humble pie.

Send out minutes. As in *Field of Dreams*, "If you build it, people will come." However, don't be offended if you do not get a huge crowd. That does not mean people are not interested. Be sure to send out your minutes to keep everyone on the same page. Possible topics include:

- How is the budget divided?
- How is the schedule completed?
- How are teachers assigned to classes?
- How are duties assigned?
- How is it determined who observes me?
- How are maintenance duties evaluated?
- How are mentors assigned?
- How are comments on report cards selected?

Quick Think

Perhaps the last puzzle piece should remain unfound.

SEVEN

Embrace the Antithesis

When speaking about reading performance on a state assessment, a principal once asserted, "If there were a correct way to instruct our students, we [his school] would already be doing it." Stands to reason that the "correct" way of accomplishing our educational tasks are few and far between.

For example, let's say a principal and his team believed that focusing on the reading strategies (making connections, inferring, that is strategy based) will make the difference for students when it comes to both the state assessment and, more importantly, developing skills necessary to be critical readers and problem solvers. Does this mean that the school leader who has taken a different approach (teaching to the state standards) is wrong?

The measure of success exists in the achievement scores. However, what if both plans resulted in similar performance? If it is possible to have two differing approaches that can yield similar results, then the realization of success or failure as it relates to our decisions (and actions) is a bit more complex with regards to our values (linked to expectations, motivations, etc.).

Remember, when a principal (or anyone for that matter) has to make a decision, he or she should first look to see if there is a technical solution—a correct way of doing something.[1] If there is, the clearest plan might be to follow it. Truth be told, sometimes the greatest decision a leader can make is to admit ignorance and reside with what has been proven to work as long as the anticipated outcome matches the original intent. However, in situations where there is no one definable "working" solution, one should look to embrace all options, thus including the antithesis of what one might believe to be valid.

Sometimes, our emotions can hinder us when it comes to the idea of embracing the antithesis. Too often, we view these options as untenable because they serve to place us (the leader) in a position of vulnerability. In the educational profession, people make their bones by knowing things. However, what might be more beneficial, and the truest form of leadership, is exploring the options associated with the situation rather than relying on any one single factor to determine a successful outcome. By checking our egos at the door, we afford ourselves (and others) the beauty of possibilities.

Secure thought with 100 percent certainty is a myth when it comes to formal culture. *Understanding that tactical negotiations lead to cultural change requires us to reconcile with the possibility of failure.* When we agree that what we most believe to be false is possible, we allow ourselves the strength of the option. Hence, we do not back ourselves into a corner, but allow flexibility to formulate all opportunities.

Language is power. The ability to communicate on so many levels of understanding is priceless. Yet there are two words that generate the thought process like no others. Those two words are *what if*. What if we had a new curriculum? What if we made the library into an inquiry media center? What if advanced-placement classes were double blocked? What if? What if? What if?

As a school leader, it may be better to know the options than to assume the answers. When presented with decisions, recognizing what you believe to be true is critical, but just as vital is our ability to know that the opposite of our beliefs is also valid, thus providing us with a measuring stick for future actions.

PRACTICAL ADVICE

Embrace the gray. If you are the type of person that only sees the black and white in situations, this may not be the job for you. When dealing with human beings and formal culture, there are going to be many times when the "correct" answers do not exist, thus forcing us to live within the gray.

For instance, the fact that the discipline book states a person receives a two-day suspension for being insubordinate does not answer the preceding question of "What does insubordination look like?" Our understanding of social situations and appropriate actions/non-actions will guide numerous conversations in a constant search for what is right for your school. See it all!

If you know there is going to be disagreement for a certain idea, start with it. Too often, when we are trying to introduce an idea, we do our best to prove our point first to secure favor. However, perhaps starting with the disagreement is a better plan. For example, if you were going to try to explain why a new schedule change is a good idea for your school, maybe starting with the reasons it is not allows the naysayers a chance to be heard. In a sense, you deflate the argument by choosing not to argue, but to acknowledge that although this is an idea, it is not the only one.

Do not surround yourself with "yes" people. Earlier in my career, I probably would not have been secure enough with myself to not only say this, but also actually want to follow it. However, with experience comes wisdom . . . and a ton of screw-ups! It is healthy to engage people who see things differently than us. As long as you both can stay focused on the goal and be respectful of each other's right to disagree, you might find that your "devil's advocate" could be your greatest ally in providing you with the "hidden" thoughts that so many may not be willing to share.

Be wary that some might not tell you the truth. Fear of reprisal is unfortunately part of informal culture. Just as parents may be resistant to emailing a teacher about an issue concerning their child, teachers may also be equally cautious to tell you something. This is not to say that you are the Big Bad Wolf. You might be one heck of a human being. But note that sometimes people get nervous to disagree with the boss. Offer opportunities for your staff to tell it like it is. We are all in this together.

I know we are true colleagues when you tell me I might be wrong.

*I know we are **true** colleagues when you tell me I might be **wrong**.*

NOTE

1. K. G. Clabaugh and G. E. Rozycki, *Understanding Schools: The Foundations of Education* (New York: Harper & Row, 1990).

EIGHT

Common Threads

Investigating and Solving School Discipline

As a new assistant principal, I can remember processing my first disciplinary issue. Margie (pseudonym) received a discipline referral for being disrespectful to a peer. I can recall reading the referral, chatting with the teacher who wrote it, and feeling pretty good about what I thought had happened.

Margie, who had been in the office quite a bit last year (so I had been told), apparently slammed her books on her desk and yelled, "Shut up!" to a girl who sat directly beside her. Simple enough. I looked at the discipline and realized the code would call for an administrative detention for being disrespectful. Again, the process seemed pretty straight forward . . . that is, until I actually chatted with Margie.

As one can imagine, Margie did not see the story quite the way the others did. In fact, there were several points that did not match the previous ones. First, Margie did not bring any books in class that day. In fact, she stated that what the teacher heard was her foot as it got caught under the desk. She also stated that she was getting tired of hearing the girl talking to her friends during class. She was merely trying to get the other students to be quiet.

In addition, she stated that the teacher was working with a student on the other side of the room when the event took place, and that he took the word of the other students over hers.

As Margie continued to chat, I feverishly took notes and began to realize that this simple disciplinary issue was not going to be as straightforward as I had anticipated. At that moment, I also realized that despite all of my formal education, despite the plethora of theories concerning human behavior, social interactions, and instructional leadership, I was never formally taught a systemic process for handling disciplinary issues. Did one even exist?

I can recall university professors skimming the topic of discipline by saying, "Use your best judgment and follow the code." And until that day with Margie, I just assumed that sound advice would be enough.

However, sloganistic statements only go so far when reality knocks and interpretation begins.

I realized that without a plan, I was lost in the translation of trying to deduce these social interactions without even a starting point. Once that happened, all of my previous moves came into question. Should I have chatted with the teacher first? Should I have brought the two girls in together? What questions should I have asked? Was I assuming truth too early?

Did my knowing that Margie had been in the office before cloud my judgment? The enormity of this outcome resided in my hands. It was my move, and people were waiting.[1]

Were you ever taught a method of investigation? Chances are, you were not. How could such a leading aspect of the principal's job be so ignored? Perhaps the answer resides in our inability to assist with indiscretion involved in investigating . . . until now.

Obviously, reading the text would be a huge benefit for anyone dealing with investigation in schools; however, here are a few points from the book to get you started in understanding how to investigate without bias.

RATIONALE

Perhaps one of the greatest challenges we face as school personnel is the necessity to suppress our personal agendas (philosophies) prior to handling any type of investigative procedure. Doing the right thing is easy, but agreeing on the right thing becomes a daunting task for educated people who possess different philosophies and procedures.

An administrator has the dual responsibility to be both the investigator and also the judge (setting consequences). One would hope that we would be able to take a clear approach when handling the issues of proper and improper behavior. However, without a formal system for investigating, we are left with only our own philosophy and a myriad of questions as it pertains to what is right.

One of the greatest aspects to any research has to do with the validity (legitimacy) of the investigative information. In order to build an authentic case, the qualitative researcher (administrator doing the investigation) must be able to evaluate various forms of data to locate the patterns within it. One can accomplish this task by utilizing member checks for responses, healthy descriptions of events, and triangulation (analyzing various points of data to locate consistencies) of all data. Once completed, the researcher will have the opportunity to identify a plausible framework to build reasonable conclusions.

ACTION STEPS

Common Threads is a methodology that guides an investigation by iso-lating facts to draw educated conclusions. It is a sequential plan designed to remove subjectivity found in accusations that arise from investigations. The process relies on six steps described by the acronym *THREAD*.

1. *T*ap your resources,
2. *H*andle incident report sheets,
3. *R*eview with an interview,
4. *E*xamine the chart,
5. *A*ddress the consequences, and
6. *D*ecide on future planning.

Incidents can occur at a school at any time. From these reports, our job as administrators is to engage in the process of investigating what happened in order to offer a resolution. Be it a student, teacher, parent, guidance counselor, or any other person that brings forth an issue that they deem to need intervention. The process of Common Threads begins as soon as an initial report occurs. From the onset, the necessity to be organized and prepared to handle the investigation is vital to the success that one will attain.

The remainder of the text defines the process, gives case studies, handouts, progressions, and so on. It is devised as a usable handbook to guide the reader through the process, and it seems like it is doing its job to help.

> As a middle school assistant principal, Common Threads is an indispensable tool that I practice daily. It is simple to use and enables me to synthesize the data in such a clear, organized way. As a result, I am better able to make good data-driven decisions and provide well-developed rationales for each. (Geoff Mills, Principal, Peirce Middle School)

PRACTICAL ADVICE

Your turn. Think about it, your primary responsibility is the instructional leader in the school, but it is also the lead investigator as well. Do yourself and your community a favor: read the book, secure the training, and be able to process the issues without bias in a systematic manner. Case closed.

Common Threads does not have to be used for just discipline. School administrators will be faced with many difficult scenarios and situations that could lend themselves to using Common Threads. Teacher investigations, parent incidents, colleague-to-colleague struggles, and day-to-day fact-finding can be completed more efficiently by incorporating Common

Threads. Like any good method, the application extends beyond the original intent.

Parents have a visible blueprint of a process. There is nothing worse than receiving an ominous call at work hearing that your child is in trouble at school. A parent's first instinct is to defend and protect. Common Threads will allow a parent to see the progression of each incident with nonbiased accuracy from witnesses and their child's own account of what transpired. Talk about establishing a team approach to discipline.

NOTE

1. A. Barber and J. Ulmer, *Common Threads: Investigating and Solving School Discipline* (Lanham, MD: Rowman & Littlefield, 2013).

NINE

What's the Win?

Consider this situation: Let's say that you have a student in grade three who is struggling with math. In pursuit of a tutor, you run into an entanglement between the union and central office when it comes to the correct amount for compensation. The district is holding tight to the contract language that states it is $40 dollars an hour for tutoring; however, the union believes that the hour is worth $50, as this was the new precedent that was set forth this past year during summer school.

Two weeks have gone by from your request with no resolution. In being the principal, what would you do?

Clearly, the ultimate win is for the child to attain the appropriate educational support. Yet in any given situation, it is also wise to consider where the win is from each side of the argument. In this circumstance, there are other issues at play—ones that happen to be out of your jurisdiction. However, what is in your control is searching for an alternative.

Perhaps there is someone who offers sessions during lunch or maybe during a breakfast club. Maybe there is a high school student that would be willing to help out or maybe even you. In not wanting to "bite the boss" or compound the issue for the union, your opinion here may not be part of a viable solution on either end.

In considering wins, we must allow our brains to go beyond what is to see what needs to be. We cannot get dragged into battles that detract us from the goal of "winning" for the students—our ultimate mission. But it is a delicate balance to negotiate when you are dealing with special-interest groups vying for resources, attention, and so forth.

One of the greatest strategists that ever walked our earth was the Chinese philosopher Sun Tzu. In his book titled *The Art of War*, he stated, "For to win one hundred victories in one hundred battles is not the acme of skill. To subdue the enemy without fighting is the acme of skill."[1] In educational terms, to enter into every scholastic skirmish only exhausts our efforts and leaves us depleted for when they truly matter.

Winning is not defined by the argument; it is defined by the non-argument but still accomplishing the same results.

In considering our opening scenario, winning is getting the student what he needs; everything else is someone else's campaign. Can you have an opinion? Sure. Give it when asked, but to enter the fray just to be right or just because you are the principal and you can is impulsive and unwise. Do not exhaust yourself with every wrangle that comes your way. Be smart and exercise your right to step aside.

When reading over the first couple drafts of this manuscript, a few of my close friends critiqued this chapter. In fact, they thought it should not be included. "You cannot compare being a principal to being at war." As a retort, I would always ask them to state a few precursors to war: disagreement, imbalance of power, rights of the individuals versus the rights of the collective, and so on.

As a principal, we sit in a position of power. And that power comes with responsibility to ourselves, the team, and the students and families. But power can be a funny thing. Power can be used to break down walls or build impenetrable forces. The goal for us must be to utilize our position to avoid the conflict but still attain the desired outcome. To accomplish this mission, sometimes we are going to win, and sometimes it will require us to lose. (Yes, it is okay to lose as the leader.) *Knowing when to lose is the mark of ingenuity.*

One way to determine your course of action when it comes to defining the win can start by considering this simple but effective proposal: *What is best for this child?* As you explore the possible answer to this question, difficult situations will start to become clear on the actions you should or should not take. As a principal, you will have various vantage points from which people will try to convince you to see "their" win. Stay firm to your central mission and always remember why we are here.

What is best for this child?

PRACTICAL ADVICE

Sometimes planned failures are a good thing. In considering the ultimate win for a child, there may be times when personal loss can provide a better win for the overall situation. For instance, you could ask someone else to assist you with finding an alternative tutor. In fact, you have already set it up but asked this person to affirm it and tie it all together. This way, they get the credit, the child gets the help, and you get the satisfaction of knowing all is well. (Every time someone else gives the big speech, everybody wins.)

Don't hesitate to ask for help. As mentioned in the last paragraph, the greatest resource we have in the education business is people. Be sure to utilize the whole team if necessary to secure a win for a student. Galaxies of possibilities exist seconds away as long as we forgo the need to control everything.

Marry the theme to the mission. In securing the central theme for the school, be sure to include a student-centered focus. Themes like "What is best for this child?" work because they compel us to keep a precise charge. Now be sure to engage the staff in creating the mission to create the glue for the team. Dream really big!

NOTE

1. Sun Tzu, *The Art of War*, trans. Lionel Giles (New York: Barnes & Noble, 2012).

TEN

You Don't Know What
You Don't Know

Darryl Smith worked for an incredible principal when he was an assistant. Dr. Connie, Darryl's boss, was generous, kind-hearted, intelligent, and an all-around fantastic human being. From observations to special education, Darryl always boasted what a tremendous resource she was.

And yet, despite her collaborative nature and willingness to involve him in leadership initiatives, he admitted there were days when his feeling of compassion toward her would wane. These weak moments usually occurred when he was attending to the discipline, and Dr. Connie was doing "other fun things."

Knowing what a benevolent person she was, Darryl truly never had any ill will toward her personally. However, there was this little voice inside him that pestered periodically. The "must be nice" phrase would start to creep into his conscious—must be nice to be able to eat lunch in peace; must be nice to have time to meet with kids, grab a coffee, write an instructional article. Must be nice!

If Dr. Connie was such a great person, and Darryl truly knew that, why did he get so upset? Why do teachers get so upset with us? Principals with central office? Why?

Society is filled with conspiracy theorists, and Darryl was one of them. You know, the type of people that think there is some predetermined life force out to thwart our best efforts. It happens all the time on every level. For instance, when you were a teacher referring to the principals, did you ever wonder, *What do they do up there all day?*

Part of this type of questioning has to deal with our own insecurities. We think, *I am working hard. Are they?* This type of "bean-counter" mentality serves to create tension and distrust.

The idea that *we don't know what we don't know* tries to serve as a leveling mechanism for our brains. Too often, we assume intention based on a philosophy and lose sight of judging the action as a standalone. For instance, when a teacher questions the whereabouts of a principal, maybe the guiding philosophy of that teacher is that the principal is avoiding his or her responsibility (judgments based on predetermined philosophy) rather than just thinking another event must have taken precedence (judgments based on needs).

Our minds want to make connections. We look for ways to "justify" these connections when it comes to creating a series of plausible thought to explain a "perceived" pattern (even if no pattern exists). In a sense, without doing the research on any particular topic, we take a mental shortcut by assuming truth as a viable option. Call it qualitative research without validity or reliability checks. In fact, call it qualitative conjecturing.

Maybe the pace of our jobs contributes to this phenomenon. Again, we are all busy; maybe the lack of time to talk creates a situation whereby we need to substitute philosophy for reality. Without making the time to do the research, we draw the perennial conclusion on a given situation. Here is where we, as human beings, falter.

Now, it would be easy to state that we all need to make more time to talk to each other to provide better understanding and trust. That would be an amazing world, but one that is not easy to create on any given day.

Therefore, we need to, at the very least, devise a way of "rearranging" our brains. Saying "I don't know what I don't know" helps gain perspective and reminds us that until we do the research, we must withhold judgment. We still might not like the current situation, but we have to force ourselves to forgo the angst that goes along with conspiracy, to dismiss the anger that goes along with treachery. We must.

PRACTICAL ADVICE

We cannot claim someone is incompetent doing a job we have never done. If a principal wants to say that an assistant principal is incompetent, I suppose he or she can make that claim due to the fact that he or she did that job. However, an assistant principal should never claim the principal is incompetent because of the lack of experience for the job—that is, you don't know what you don't know! Now, as the assistant, you may not agree with the manner in which the principal is doing the job, but without actually sitting in the big chair, claiming incompetency shows our ignorance.

Why are we so afraid of being labeled as incompetent for asking questions? Think about it: we all went to school and gained our respective degrees; however, those degrees certainly did not cover every possible educational topic. In being an administrator, there are times when we have to be a generalist and rely on the experts around us. Search for opportunities to learn new ideas with earnest, and people will respect your genuine desire. Better to plead ignorance and solicit input than to demonstrate arrogance by pretending to know what we do not.

Sometimes, the "other fun things" are not that much fun. Years later, Darryl became a middle school principal of the same school where he worked for Dr. Connie. It turns out those "other fun things" that Dr. Connie was attending to were now Darryl's responsibility. Ironically, Darryl sometimes wishes he was involved in a juicy investigation instead of dealing with a contract issue or testifying at the next arbitration hearing. Turns out the principal's job has a few undesirable components to it, just as the assistant's job does. Funny how that goes.

Quick Think

Conception is the first spark of initiative.

ELEVEN

The New Competition

Oftentimes we are faced with competitive situations that require us to dig deep into our reserve to create a winning situation for ourselves. In these instances, we push ourselves to extreme degrees to satisfy that internal (self-accomplishment) or external motivation (rewards) that drives us to success.

However, too often in today's PC society, we are coerced into situations where the competition is replaced by a teamwork model. Now, on the surface, who could argue with the concept of teamwork? For example, let's say that you own a company that makes umbrellas. It seems quite logical if you were to be introduced to a competitor that wanted to join forces with you, the newly established team might be able to accomplish so much more together than alone.

But what if the companies had to be separate but exactly the same? Would we be able to maintain the motivation if we were mandated to concede our internal/ external drives?

In situations that require us to "exact" ourselves to another, we sometimes have a tendency to embrace the least common attribute for fear of exposing our partner's weaknesses or being made to seem that we are not team players. *In these situations, we eliminate competition in the name of team; however, the new competition becomes consistency.* In other words, we "force" ourselves into a "lock-step" type of mentality. One place where this situation plays out is in our school systems.

In school districts that have multiple schools within a system (e.g., two high schools, three middle schools, etc.), the schools are likely to receive a mandate to provide the "same" experience for students regardless of where they attend. Zip code should not dictate the educational experience. Right?

Once again, the principle appears logical. However, what if the conditions were right for one school to create a miraculous illumination with a specific topic? If we have been mandated for consistency, these opportunities can sometimes be squashed due to the inability of the other schools to carry out a certain initiative. Likewise, just because the conditions (personal, location, support mechanism, etc.) were not right for one school does not provide an airtight rationale for another school not to soar. To assume exactness diminishes the role of culture in our systems—a gigantic myth.

Within these situations, perhaps it is okay for one school to extend itself beyond the norm to drive the others to greatness. Perhaps competition in these instances can be a good thing, as it has the ability to push our thinking and outputs. Maybe experience (be it in a school setting or other venue) has as much to do with the conditions (context) as it does with an initial premise of consistency.

Teamwork should not be abandoned. In fact, teamwork is a critical component in our lives. Yet we need to recognize that competition is present even within the greatest of teams, and it is okay to create that healthy environment.

PRACTICAL ADVICE

Do not place yourself or others into situations that compromise their individual potential in the name of consistency. As you view your situations as they relate to this concept, think about the structure of consistency. Is there some way to offer a variety of choice to extend one's ability to increase their internal motivation instead of solely relying on external ones (forced uniformity)?

Build choice and promote chance. In realizing that a little healthy competition can spur us on to greatness, it is the role of the principal to create these chances for our teams to soar. Obviously, if one team is trying to "outdo" another for the sake of completion, then that situation must be rectified. Allowing our teams to experiment with their passions provides us a glimpse into the human spirit—what better message to send our students than this!

Don't wage war on the innocent in the name of justice. If you work for a boss that disagrees with this premise, it is not advisable to take him or her on by using the team as the army. Even though you may have an idea that could work (correct—technical culture), remember the boss has the authority to dictate against it. Running pilot after pilot when you know the answer is going to be no only drains the team and sets up dissention between you, the staff, your boss, and so forth. If you do not like your boss's decision, then take the steps to be the boss (and be sure to read the previous chapter again).

TWELVE

The Fives Test

As we look at very difficult decisions or situations that may confront us, it is easy to see why so many of us either chose to just not make a decision in light of the perceived consequences or simply put off the decision with the wish that it will somehow magically take care of itself. Be it procrastination or complete denial, the situation, much like an old penny, will still be sitting in the same place where you dropped it . . . more worn, more weathered, and still in need of attention.

The fives test gives us a quick opportunity to take our decision and analyze it between the two forces that most matter in any situation—impact and time. For example, let's say that you are in a job that you just cannot stand. Now, let's compound the issue by stating that this job, your sole source of income, had once been your dream job. In fact, all of your education has led you to this "dream" job, only to find out that it is certainly not what you had expected.

How many people do you know that exist in this realm, day in and day out, only to suffer, complain, or muddle their way through?

We have all faced this perceived mountain. "Should I quit? Do I stay? I feel helpless. What will I do?" These and other questions swirl around us like scattered papers in a wind storm. We hope for the "gale" to pass, and ultimately, it does. But we know in our hearts the bad weather is coming again, and it will continue to get worse each occurrence.

By accepting a powerless state, we lock ourselves into the habitual act of complaining without action. So what can we do? The first decision that has to be made is that in any situation, the only entity that we can control is ourselves. Let me say that again: *the only entity that we can control is ourselves.* And here is where the fives test helps us see it clearly. Let's review our job example to see how it works.

51

If you opted to quit your job, how would you feel five seconds afterward? How about five minutes after? Five hours? Five days, weeks, months, years? Get the point? Let's analyze this premise utilizing the following graph with impact and time:

Impact of Attitude

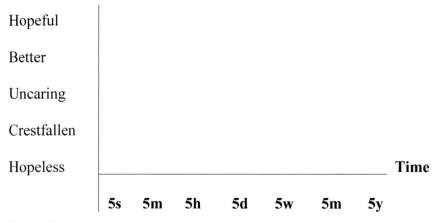

Figure 12.1.

"If I quit my job, at what point would I start to feel better (impact axis) about the situation in relation to time (the fives)? In other words, if I am miserable now, could I guess at what point I would not be so miserable?"

As one can see, the "potential" to feel differently about the job if you decide to look for another job has merit. Meaning, if you "do something" about your situation, the chance to change your impact exists because *you have taken control of your situation.*

Impact of Attitude

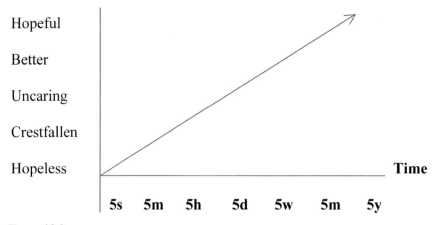

Figure 12.2.

Conversely, if we take another line and represent that as *doing nothing* (i.e., just remaining in your job), you can see that the potential for impact in a positive direction is not necessarily within your sole control:

Impact of Attitude

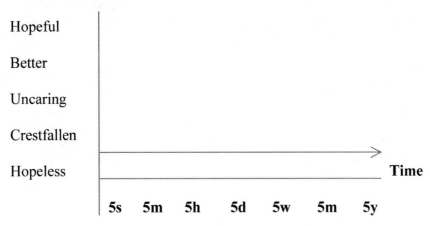

Figure 12.3.

In addition, if you decide that you are going to change your attitude about your job based on the risk factor of simply quitting it, you still have to come to the realization that to change the impact, you must take control of your situation. By simply doing nothing and "waiting" for aspects of your job to change or the job itself or people involved with it, you are breeding helplessness and a spiraling sense of doom.

Impact of $

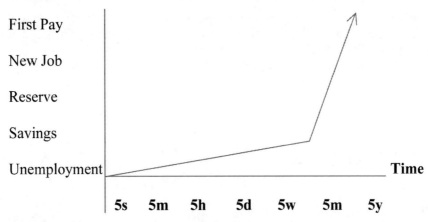

Figure 12.4.

Of course, one may say that one might feel "better" about not being in this job, but certainly would not feel great overall without another job.

Agreed. And that is the tipping point of the decision that the individual must resolve. Perhaps another five to see when I could expect to attain a new job could assist me with my decision.

If one truly believed that one could find a new job in less than five months, perhaps the risk to try and the potential for happiness could enable one to make that change that so desperately resides within during both our weak and strong moments.

PRACTICAL ADVICE

"If you chose not to decide, you still have made a choice." One of my favorite song lyrics of all time comes from the band Rush. (Yes, I'm old.) However, despite my age, this adage resonates with many a situation. Too often, we allow ourselves to sit on the sidelines of a decision. Take initiative and choose an option rather than succumbing to the ineptitude of the unresolved.

Use the fives both in and out of school. This strategy does not have to be limited to simply school-related issues. The fives test works well with many decisions that ask us to consider time and impact. Do not feel weird grabbing a napkin and a pencil to chart out the fives. Better to see the possibilities than turn a blind eye toward them.

Principal as counselor, use the fives. Although we are the instructional leaders of our buildings, principals assume various roles throughout the course of time. One of those roles is therapist. Similar to a guidance counselor, staff, other administrators, and even parents may look to confide in you for support or advice. One of the best strategies we can provide to our team is the ability to look at a given situation with patience and a clear mind. The fives depersonalizes the advice by simply channeling the other person's situation into a perceivable one. The principal then becomes a guide rather than an omnipotent being. Teach people to fish.

Remember what if. Recall the accounts of the prior chapters. Conception is the first spark of initiative. Begin with the possibilities. Make your reality. Think it; do it!

Quick Think

Define your passions; cling to them as if they were the air you breathe.
For in a sense, they are just that.

THIRTEEN

On Saving Face

Ted was an exceptional teacher. Students loved him, the staff respected him, and the entire community sang his praises. Janice, being the principal of the building, had always felt honored to have him on the staff. Ted was brilliant at his craft and known throughout the middle school as being a most positive person. He coached everything, volunteered for countless committees, and always had a smile on his face.

When Ted went to see Janice one day with a despondent look on his face, she knew something was up. Ted explained that the band director's job was about to open at their high school. Ted, in being a life-time "middle school guy," had never taught in the high school. Although he loved the middle school and the dynasty he had built, his passion was calling. Ted wanted to be the band director at the high school, and he needed the principal's help.

After Ted left the office, Janice just sat there for a few moments. She did not want to lose him, but told him she would do everything she could to make his dream come true. As the principal, you are going to see great ones come and go. You have to accept that and appreciate the time they are with you. Always think, *Better to have a dynamic teacher for a few years than to have a mediocre one for thirty!*

As the spring staffing meeting commenced, Janice entered with a mission—help Ted get to the high school. During the meeting, she jockeyed for position. (Staffing meetings can be tense if you are not prepared.) Luckily, an opportunity arose. Ted could go to the high school, but Janice was going to have to send extra staffing to the high school to make the schedule work. Yikes! What a decision. Help Ted and raise class size for others or hold tight knowing that she could have done something, but did not. After a few moments, Janice knew what needed to be done. She held true to her promise and sanctioned Ted's transfer to the high school.

The next day, Ted was asked to come to the office. When Janice told him the news, the man cried with joy. (He literally cried with tears of joy.) She told him how much the school was going to miss him. As was his humble nature, he thanked Janice. As he turned to leave, she asked him if he wanted her to inform the staff. Janice had realized it might be tough for him and wanted to help out. He said "no thank you" and left the office.

"Wow! That was a cool moment" thought Janice.

And that joy lasted all of fifteen minutes. For as soon as Janice walked into the hallway, she was bombarded by two team leaders with glaring eyes.

"How could you?" the one said with such disdain. Janice could hardly believe her ears.

"Excuse me?" she said.

"After all that man has done for this school," the other one retorted.

Dazed and confused, Janice asked for clarification. And what came next was her indoctrination into the role of the principal. After Ted had left the office, he went straight down to the seventh-grade lunchroom and proceeded to tell the staff that the principal "shipped him" to the high school.

Needless to say, when Janice heard the news, she was in shock. "Ted? Ted did this? The guy she just helped. How the heck could this be?" Turns out, Ted needed a scapegoat, and Janice was his mark. True story.

Sometimes as the principal, you are going to have to take the hit for things you didn't do. On this day, it was too difficult for Ted to let his friends of twenty-some years know he wanted to leave them. It was just easier to tell a *little* white lie. He goes out a hero, and Janice plays the scoundrel. Sign, sealed, delivered.

Janice did want to set the record straight. She wanted to march right out there and start telling everyone the truth. But she didn't. Nobody wins a fight, especially when it is with teachers and administrators. So she let it roll and wished him well on his last day. They never spoke of the incident, nor did Janice ever formally address it in public. And to this day, his picture still hangs in the school lobby.

The only secure thing about life is that we are all insecure.

In not wanting to disappoint, Ted did what he had to do with regards to his security in himself. We, as the leaders of the building, must embrace the feelings of insecurity during the difficult moments. When parents are yelling, when bosses are demanding, when teachers are complaining, we must be secure in our insecurity. Times of emotion call for our brains, not more emotion.

There will be times (many times) when you are going to take undeserved blame. And your gut reaction is to let the truth be known. Do yourself a favor and take a day, two days, a week, and let it be. (Use the fives.) Do not enter into a defensive posture right out of the gate. That will present you in a negative light. Try to take the high road. Sometimes your silence will say it all.

PRACTICAL ADVICE

Find the silver lining in every situation. Was it a positive that Ted told everyone the principal shipped him out? At first, Janice could not see any silver lining. However, after a few days, one of the team leaders approached Janice and said that news of the move had really stirred people into action. Even some of the habitual late-to-work folks were getting themselves in early! They said, "If that can happen to Ted, it can certainly happen to me." Now, a principal should never condone fear tactics, but it wasn't upsetting that a few folks were *encouraged* to action.

There are ways to let the truth be known, later. After reviewing this incident, it may have been thought that Ted had done damage to the principal's rapport with the staff. In wanting to repair it, Janice did *whisper* to a few folks the true story once Ted had left the building. Although never spoken about in a formal setting, she was pretty confident that these people would at least share the truth. Was it smart? Should she have just let it go? Probably. But maybe her insecurity needed the boost. Such is life.

Remember the safety walks. When occasions like this one occur, best to take a walk. Clear your brain. Get some fresh air. Go grab a coffee. Do what you have to do to compose yourself. As the leader, we must refrain from losing our cool in public. Take some time to process the event. Look at it from all stakeholders' point of view. *Process.* That should be your reaction.

The problems come in their time; the answers can come in yours.

FOURTEEN

Don't Bite the Boss

You wanted to be the principal. You took countless courses, spent the money, did the time. You went through interview after interview, and you finally got the job. Congratulations! You did it. All that hard work paid off. But wait a minute. Think for a moment. Besides you, what other person do you owe a hand of gratitude? What other person most likely went through every interview with you? Spoke on your behalf? Shook your hand when you finally got the job. Well?

Just as you did a ton of work to get to this point, so did your boss. Consider this, when the committee was trying to decide on the final candidate to take to the school board, do you think your boss was in your corner? Chances are, the boss saw something in you that said you would be a good fit in the job. Perhaps it was your ability to lead or your passionate enthusiasm or your commitment to results. Whatever the reasons, the boss wanted you, and now that you have the job, you are a part of the team—the team that the boss put together. So what is the issue?

As a principal, you are going to hire teachers. What type of person are you going to be hiring? What qualities would you want them to possess? Would you want someone who can help foster a team approach, assist with your vision planning? Or would you want a maverick, a real gunslinger whose off-the-cuff behaviors and disregard for authority make him a perfect target for "most likely to chat with human resources?"

When it comes to the hiring process, we are not looking for drones; however, we are searching for teammates. Now remember the qualities your boss desired in you. Just as you would want a team player, so too does your boss.

It is amazing how many principals forget this concept when they get the job. It is like they become the chief and all bets are off when it comes to team. The same administrators who become infuriated when teachers want to shut their doors are the very same folks who stop at nothing to keep central office out of their schools. Why?

Here is where the personal pronouns (my school, my staff) start to discourage the team approach between you and your boss. *Your team, as a principal, must include your boss.* Period. You are the principal; but the boss is still responsible for more in the organization. Cutting the boss out of the team only results in bitter feelings and distrust, which can lead to reprimands or worse.

Therefore, it is not all right to make fun of your boss in public or through email. It is not all right to blame central office for every woe of the district. It is not all right to set up an "us-versus-them" mentality when it comes to central and the building. Got it? *Principals who lead through bargaining or playing central as the enemy wind up being really good assistant principals somewhere else.*

In being administrators, we want to be confident in what we are doing, but not cocky. If you fell in a black hole on the way to work, the school would open. The kids would learn, and we would find a new principal. Don't play God. Appreciate what you have while you have it.

Don't bite the boss. Follow this simple maxim during your tenure, and chances are you will have a very successful stay.

PRACTICAL ADVICE

When you don't agree, do it in private. It is okay to disagree with your boss, but it is foolish to fight a public battle. When you have a disagreement, talk about it. Reason with each other (if possible). Once that time passes, it is incumbent on you to be a good team player. Remember, would you want a teacher to stand up in a faculty meeting and blatantly disagree/challenge you?

Always assume the role of the professional. Even if your boss acts like a raving madcap, you must keep your cool. If your boss is unprofessional, then you will have to decide whether or not to report him or her. Only you will be able to make that decision, as one's integrity yardstick cannot be dictated by another. Furthermore, if you should lose respect for your boss, you may have to decide whether or not you want to stay in that situation. However, whacking him behind his back (or in front of him) only makes you look cowardly or appear like you are hiding something.

Find someone you can complain to outside of your district. Use your husband or wife. Find a colleague somewhere far away that you really trust. If you simply cannot take it and have to complain about your boss, do it with someone outside of your school system. "These walls have ears" (Dionysius of Syracuse).

Practice the same with your staff. Here, you are the boss. Be sure to afford your staff the very same opportunities you would want from yours. Be respectful. Agree with enthusiasm; disagree with assurance. Offer an open-door policy. Let it be known that it is okay to disagree in an appropriate manner. People want to be heard . . . so listen well.

Quick Think

The most expensive things in life start out for free.

FIFTEEN

The "Buy In" Is Out!

Jacob was a middle school principal who was also serving as the district's 6–12 math coordinator. (Yes, it happens in budget-crunch times.) For the past several months, the math teachers had been participating in a review of textbooks. The team had limited their choices to three and the deadline for recommendation was approaching

Jacob, who was a former math teacher, had a "real feel" for what he thought the team should recommend; however, the team was truly leaning toward a different selection. At a principals' meeting, when asked how the process was going, Jacob replied, "Very well. I just need to get the buy in for the right text, but that should not be a problem."

Interestingly, no one questioned his notion of buy in—partly because the other principals were not familiar with the intricacies of the situation (the team's position) and partly because the notion of "but in" is so common in upper management, no one flinched.

Jacob, being a "passionate" leader, was able to *convince* the team to select his text. These are the same books that sit neatly on the windowsills of many a math teacher's room across the district.

As a principal (or curriculum leader in this example), it is easy to want what we want. Being placed in a position of leadership, our rank dictates the ability to make critical decisions. And in situations where we have added expertise (Jacob being a former math teacher), the path for decisions appears all the more clear. Yet, as we continue to review example after example, we begin to realize attaining "buy in" is a myth.

Making decisions based on rank is the prerogative of the leader, yet many times, these types of decisions lead us into the abyss of action. Making decisions based on power (negotiated or informed) is certainly more viable and less damaging to the overall culture of the team. For instance, the option that Jacob was going to be able to "convince" the team to see it his way was not necessarily grounded in the thoughts and feelings of the team, but of himself and his position (rank).

If, however, he would have been willing to negotiate the point, perhaps if he could have run a pilot or even just explained the rationale and provide the data to support his stance, the long-term impact on the team (and their use of the text) might have been better.

As administrators, why do we feel the need to "daddy" everyone? I realize that our hides are on the line when it comes to making critical decisions. Many think, *The buck stops with me—if I am going to be held accountable, I am going to make the decisions.* Yet there may be a fault with this line of thinking.

For instance, do you want your boss to select your hires? Seriously, would you want your supervisor selecting all of your teachers? Would this work for you? I know this would bother the heck out of me. If I am going to be responsible for these folks day in and day out, I would want the say in the hiring. Sound reasonable? If so, return to the original scenario with Jacob. If the teachers are going to have to "work with" the math books day in and day out, shouldn't they be afforded the same control as you with your hires?

Control freaks burn out. Plus, they do not understand the Theory of Relevance. Jacob may have an opinion about the texts, but ultimately, the group that is more relevant in this situation is the teachers. They are the ones that have to "live" by the decision. We all realize if the math program fails, Jacob would have to account for its demise, but so too would the staff. They are not going to select a text that they feel will fail—theory of relevance signifies a learned selection.

The buck does stop here; however, what we need to do as principals is understand that the word *here* includes everyone. Building a culture of collaboration shares the ownership in given instances, allowing for a greater voice to be given by all peoples.

PRACTICAL ADVICE

Get the power. I realize it sounds strange to say, but as a leader you may have the rank, but what you need is the power. And you want the power in order to give it away. You cannot force "buy in" on someone, but you certainly can set the stage for ownership, which fosters personal "buy in." One can utilize pilots, check-ins, and other methods of supervision to ensure all is well; yet the name of the game is shared action.

If you are planning to convince people of your point, you have already lost. In times of peace, allowing people to give input to any decision secures (at the very least) trust in a process. Once a decision is made, share it. Explain your rationale and reasoning, but there is not a necessity to convince people. That would have come during the discussion leading up to the decision. Trying to convince people after the fact only builds mistrust that the original platform was tampered with. Conversely, in times of crisis, make decisions based on your training. Here, you have every right to take the lead.

Delegate effectively. If you know someone is not capable of handling the responsibility of a decision, tell them. Do not compromise the process by substituting scenarios for lack of understanding. Be smart. Honesty results in a better acceptance of the decision than planning to "assist" someone with a decision they cannot make in the first place.

The Theory of Relevance. Responsibility for the outcome of an action resides in various stakeholders, especially in the school system. Oftentimes, people of rank try to influence folks to their way of thinking. The Theory of Relevance asks us to establish the greatest exposure to the actual decision and adjust power accordingly. This is not to say that the person of rank cannot ultimately make the final call, but to disregard the people closest to the impact often leads to the non-action. If "they" have to use your decision, then it's best to see what "they" think.

SIXTEEN

Rock and Roll

Music is a part of our history. Some would say it defines us as a people, especially today. Look around the gym or grocery store. Everyone has an iPod! We are the plugged-in generation, and for my money, no musical genre does it better than good old rock and roll.

Rock and roll has variation. They don't call it "rock and rock." Sometimes you rock, and sometimes you roll. But put the two halves together, and we have the yin- and the yang-covered cheesy ballad or hip-shaking shimmy; rock and roll has it all.

One of the finest educational books I have ever come across is *School and Society* by Feinberg and Soltis. Within the pages of this text, the authors identify the relationship between school and society by capturing the essence of how schools operate and how we (the people) react to the system.

Feinberg and Soltis speak of three schools of thought—*functionalist* (school functions to teach us how to live in society—focusing on the rights of the collective), *conflict theorist* (school serves to keep the majority in power—focusing on the rights of the individual), and *interpretivist* (school depends—focusing on the argument at hand not a global philosophy like functionalist or conflict theorists).[1]

For the benefit of our conversation, let's think of these theories as human beings. A functional person sees the world as black or white. To him, fair is equal. If he were a baseball umpire, the strike zone would be consistent (his knees to chest) for everyone regardless of who they are.

Conversely, a conflict theorist does not consider fair as equal. As an umpire, the strike zone would favor the underdogs because the rules of the game support the favorites.

An interpretivist umpire's strike zone might fluctuate based on the needs of the team and the individual. This umpire would not concern himself with fair or equal because *fair depends on the situation*. Tall batters, short batters, winner, and losers would get what they needed based on the standard of the game. The interpretivist umpire would not call balls or strikes based on who they believed should win or lose, but on the needs and standards of the moment.

How does this research fit into our conversation? One of the greatest factors that influence our system sometimes goes without ever being mentioned in the conversation. That factor is the system itself. Examine people's place within the system and sometimes we can learn more about ourselves and the pressures that are placed on us to secure the needs of all. (What we might view as personal may not be.)

In our schools, teachers can often take the form of functionalists. Their jobs ask them to service students *many to one*. In other words, most teachers look to the needs of the group with relation to the needs of the individuals within the group. Stands to reason.

Teachers deal with many students at one time and are sometimes forced into a "fair is equal" approach just by sheer numbers. It is not unlikely for a teacher to explain, "If I do that for you, Johnny, I would need to do that for everyone else." Not necessarily the answer Johnny was looking for, but one that he can somewhat understand. Teachers establish norms they can achieve for everyone.

Although some of my colleagues would scoff at the later example, and state that teachers need to "go above and beyond for each child," we cannot diminish the system's expectations on a teacher. It is not easy servicing fifteen to twenty to thirty students per class per period, when a third or more may have Individual Education Programs (IEPs). (Explain that to your dinner friends.)

On the other hand, guidance counselors, school psychologists, special education teachers, and so on, play a different role in the system. These folks view the system from the needs of the *one to many* (conflict theorists). Their day-to-day tasks place them in a position of designee, whereby the individual elicits the attention. The one child's needs trump that of the masses or the necessity to have consistency among them. When writing an IEP, classroom implications do not precede individual expectations. It is all about this child, the one-to-many mantra!

The principal sits right in the middle of these two worlds. It is our task to balance the rights of the individuals and the rights of the collective. In a sense, we are asked to "interpret" situations as they reside between the two philosophies. Pretty cool!

The key point to any decision between the individual and the collective is to eliminate bias. To do this, we must arrive at each action as a standalone and not part of a past philosophy that is guiding our thinking. For example, suppose a student is in the office waiting to see you about a bullying incident. Suppose a teacher brought the child to you with that accusation. Now add to it that this child has bullied others before. Would that make him guilty of this next incident?

In eliminating bias, we must not pass judgment based on prior action or a belief system that would assume innocence or guilt prior to the action. If we took a functional point of view, the student in this case is guilty—where there is smoke, there's fire.

A functionalist would be concerned about the rights of the bullied as opposed to the bully. A conflict theorist might garner the child's innocence based on the belief that the "system" is corrupt—"they always have it out for this child." With this position, the individual's needs would outweigh the masses.

The smart move is to take an interpretivist stance, whereby we waive a decision until we have investigated thoroughly. By determining the most logical sequence of events (the circumstances that define the action), we can move to judgment without the pangs of conscience that arrive when we assume truth without knowledge. (Revisit the "Common Threads" chapter.)

As one considers these educational concepts and the complexity that they could bring to one's conscience, think of Credence Clearwater "rolling on a river." Maybe the best plan of action is to realize sometimes we will need to be on the side of the collective (rock), and others times we will need to support the individual (roll). That is the essence of the position. That is the ultimate role of the principal. Avoiding predetermined philosophical judgments assists us in limiting prejudice and fostering a better sense of justice for all.

PRACTICAL ADVICE

Share this information with the staff. Whether we enjoy it or not, it may be easier to work for a functionalist boss or a conflict-theory one. With both of these approaches, we can sort of know which way decisions are going to fall based on past precedent. It is not easy, however, to work for an interpretivist, one that has no predetermined direction (only that of assisting the child). By sharing this information, perhaps you can build a conversation and language among the team to foster understanding during decision times—a perfect "How does that work?" topic!

Be wary of conspiracy theorists. A conspiracy theorist has a predetermined thought process by which he or she judges events (whether facts are known or not). Openings like "I know what happened" prior to any investigation present a false assumption of power, placing the theorist "in the know." Most times, when you really analyze a conspiracy theorist, he or she is usually a functionalist or conflict theorist at heart. Do your best to know who these folks are. Try to have them attend a think session on the topic. Maybe they will see their pattern. Maybe not. At least the attempt was made.

Locate the balance in whatever you are doing. Even in the most black-and-white situations (e.g., reading through a discipline code of conduct — rights of the collective) there are going to be checks to the system to allow the principal to keep the balance (within the discipline code, sentences like "The information in this book is a guide; the administrator has the right to interpret these guidelines the way he or she sees fit" — rights of the individual). Highlight these circumstances when reviewing guidelines with the staff. This way, when a decision does go "against" what someone would have assumed, you can explain with confidence.

They don't call it "rock and rock"!

NOTE

1. W. Fienberg and F. J. Soltis, *School and Society* (New York: Teachers College Press, 1998).

SEVENTEEN

My Miracle

Of all the goals you have accomplished, of every summit you have climbed and conquered, what do you think is the greatest thing you have ever done? Some in our profession would point to earning lofty degrees; others might share a story about a struggling student whom we were able to reach. Whatever the event, these milestones serve as a reminder of why we wanted to be in education and motivate us for our next pinnacle.

In being reflective, how do you think our students' parents would answer the same question?

In dealing with a discipline situation, a principal friend of mine, Donna, once had a parent who lost her mind. Obviously, Donna had other occurrences where parents had become disturbed, but never to the degree that this parent did. Regardless of the specifics, the parent truly felt that her son was being harassed by a teacher.

Truth be told, it was a mutual situation, and one that was handled on both ends. However, during the "discussion," this mother said something that has always remained. In referring to her son, she stated, "This is my miracle!" And at that moment, Donna knew she would never forget this valuable lesson.

When we are involved with school situations, sometimes it is easy for us to forget that the child in front of us is someone's miracle. On that particular day, my friend remembered this issue was her fourth in a series of about twelve. She was tired and a bit put off, and can honestly admit she was rushing. This woman could sense her frustration and assumed that her demeanor was a reflection on her child and not on the ongoings of her day. Donna had forgotten.

There is an enormous difference between getting something done and getting it done well.

In this instance, Donna had neglected to demonstrate her compassion and understanding that would come with working with someone's miracle. She should have taken a walk or gone to get a glass of water. But she did not.

When dealing with our families, it is critical to see things from the parent's perspective. Think about it: with a typical discipline incident, the parent is home or at work. They have a host of issues they are dealing with on their own, and then we call them with our news.

It is natural from them to be startled and get defensive—they are hearing about how "their miracle" did something wrong. Sometimes, they look on this event as a reflection on their parenting. Other times, a parent might recollect to their days in school and transpose their experiences (positive or negative) into the current situation.

When dealing with families, we must remember that each child is someone's miracle. This does not excuse behaviors, but only looks to serve as a barometer on how we are approaching the situation. This type of passionate methodology is often the center of various student resolution models, but can also serve as a guide for all interactions.

PRACTICAL ADVICE

Stay calm. People are going to yell at you in this job. It is just going to happen, no matter how compassionate you are. Do not take it personally. Stay in control and allow the person to talk it out. Do not raise your voice, for that never bodes well when your boss learns of it (even if the person deserved it). Plus, you want to show your staff that you are always in control, no matter how hot the issues get. Stay calm. Listen. Talk slowly.

Staff members are miracles too. Interestingly, just as the children are their parent's miracles, our staff also has family that holds them in lofty regard. When dealing with issues that could cause people to get upset, set the stage for compassion by recalling the initial premise. Follow the golden rule. Even when you are involved in a dismissal, do it with compassion and dignity. Always be the professional.

Do not pass judgment in your dealings with people. In our position, there will be times when we have to judge the actions of people; however, we are not asked to judge the people. Even in the worst situations, staying to the facts and allowing a non-bias process to commence and conclude will provide the leader with a security of the staff members as being fair. We are not required to be friends with everyone we work with, but starting with an impartial stance serves the greater good beyond the incident.

Quick Think

Everything in life is compared to what.
Defining the what *is the essence of a learned life.*

EIGHTEEN

They Have Forgotten Where They Are From

Dr. Vincent Mill, a high school principal, was very excited about a new idea. Having just attended the annual conference on student achievement, he was "energized" about a new way to progress-monitor students as it related to literacy. Although the plan was initially started at the elementary level, he believed that with a few quick modifications, he would be able to institute the new procedures with relative ease.

Upon meeting with the staff, he explained how each teacher would keep a mini-journal for each student. Within the journal (online), accurate data (test scores, standardized assessment scores, etc.) would be recorded and reviewed on a biweekly basis with each grade-level administrator. Of course teachers would have to learn the online system, but how difficult could that be?

Having six classes and over 170 students, tenth-grade English teacher Colin James asked Dr. Mill a question: "Will we be getting more time to complete this work, as our time is already being utilized to plan for class, grade the weekly writing assessments, participate in academic chats, run cultural advisory, and perform our school-based duties?"

Dr. Mill's initial response was "This is good for kids." He continued his justification by stating that everyone, including himself, had to embrace the accountability that comes with continuous improvement. As Dr. Mill spoke, the staff tuned out, realizing that "one more thing" was upon them once again.

At that moment, Colin turned to his grade-level partners at his table and whispered, "He's forgotten where he's from . . . again."

"They have forgotten where they are from" has to be one of the most widely used clichés describing administrators and their relationship to staff. I would assume that most of us have either used this term or at least been in earshot of someone else verbalizing their frustration with a given situation. And on the surface, it does appear that Dr. Mill has forgotten what it is like to be a teacher (by adding on more work to an overloaded plate). However, when we truly examine this situation (and cliché), maybe the opposite better defines the scene.

What if we argued that Dr. Mill has not forgotten what it is like to be a teacher, but is doing the exact same thing he did as one?

Could that be possible? As a teacher, we assign work to students. The students, most times, do not dictate the type or amount of the work. A student may have work in one class, receive work from others, and think to herself, "There is not enough time in the day to finish all of this." Sounds a lot like the student may think the teachers have—you guessed it—forgotten what it was like to be a student.

Students often feel like this, although the word selection describing the teacher usually is not stated so politically correct as "they have forgotten what it is like." A principal, having learned about teachers "piling it on," may be inclined to have a conversation with them—explain the rationale behind homework and ask to see if the connections to higher-order thinking and relevance were present. In doing so, the principal may even appeal to a homework guideline or policy that may give specific amounts/timeframes to assist us from overburdening the students. For adults, there does not seem to be such a guideline.

People outside the teaching profession might argue that getting more work is "part of the deal" of working. Maybe it is, but does it have to be this way? As a principal, sometimes you will not have control to assist your staff in defining what they have to do (central office initiatives); however, when it comes to building actions, control is exactly what you should use when thinking about assigning "one more thing."

The feeling of helplessness is created by a lack of control. In addition, people may want very much to do a great job, only to be challenged on how to accomplish the goal with so much to do. We, as leaders, deflate motivation when we assign new tasks without rational thought, relevance, and a chance to provide input into the process.

Here is where the strategic-planning process has enormous merit. When leaders utilize a plan, one that was developed by various stakeholders, they bring a sense of confidence to the team by establishing the goals earlier in the process. Teachers then have an understanding of the expectations and can plan for the action steps accordingly. It is within the planning process itself where leaders can first establish a team approach rather than top-down management.

PRACTICAL ADVICE

You cannot do what you did as a teacher and succeed. People who do not adjust to the nuances between being a teacher and now being an administrator fail. Although positioned in the same building, they can be vastly different. We sometimes rely on past success to provide for future ones. Although success can breed success, the situations and circumstances garner the need to adjust. For example, just because your "zany sense of humor" endeared you to your students as a teacher, that does not necessarily mean it will translate to the staff in the same manner.

Utilize a mentor. A mentor is important and can be either your boss or a colleague from another district; find someone with whom you can share your thoughts. It is critical to have a person that understands similar situations through practicality. Tap into his or her knowledge base and learn from the experience.

Take something away. Education is always soliciting the next great wave. In trying to find nirvana, it is critical to also remember that as initiatives come, so too they go. Rather than getting the reputation for the "next big thing" principal, assist the staff with prioritizing what is important. Plan well and see into the future with guided presence. And measure your initiatives by the volume of the impact for both the staff and the students. Recall the story of the dog with the bone in its mouth staring at the water.

It is okay to give work. Do not be afraid to give the staff work. That is part of our job. Just be sure it is valid, practical, and community driven. If built with this format, and designed for student success, most will be okay with it. Most.

NINETEEN

The Union with the Union

Sally, the union representative in her building, had a great way about her. During most days, she would sit and chat with her principal about life, children, politics, or whatever was the hot topic of the week. Conversations were spirited, and the two would always have a good laugh. On occasion, there would be issues going on in the school that would need to be discussed. On those days, Sally or her principal would tap each other with their famous line, "Got time for business?" And at that, they would head to the office to chat.

During the business meetings, nothing was personal. She had a job to do, and so did her principal. This was not to say that they were against each other. Both understood that during these meetings, they might not agree on every issue and that was okay. As one would expect, there were good meetings and ones were they agreed to disagree. For those occasions, other folks were brought into the resolution (district office, human resources, union leadership). Frequently, they were able to figure it out to avoid the masses.

One of the greatest resources a principal has is the bond that comes with working well with your union leadership. We, as leaders, cannot see the union as "the enemy," but as an entity that was put into place to keep the balance of that system (management and worker). Those that resent the concept always seem to have issues with their people—consistently arguing point for point. A good union relationship is just that—a good relationship. There are gives and takes. (They don't call it "rock and rock.")

Often the problem with unions and management is that the issues become personal. People sometimes can personalize the agenda rather than seeing it as Sally and her principal did—it's just business. The personal components of any argument often lead to emotion. In times where you feel that you are about to lose your cool, it is critical to take time to calm down.

As we are all aware, the manner in which we handle situations can and does become greater than the situation itself, especially when the situation is mismanaged. Just as students will sometimes do things to get "under the skin" of the teacher they do not respect, so too can adults replicate this behavior. This is not to imply that unions or principals would be vindictive; however, without a solid relationship, every little thing could become an issue.

As the leader, it is our responsibility to gain trust from the staff. When we treat people with respect, when we are fair, when we tell the truth and do what we say we are going to do, we build a cache of confidence.

A goal of a principal that is certainly attainable is to never be grieved and lose. A grievance occurs when the teachers feel that an administrator has done something against the contract. Staff members can grieve anything, but with a strong relationship with the union leaders, frivolous issues are dismissed prior to even getting to you. And the ones that do hit your desk can be cooperatively discussed to look for a win-win.

PRACTICAL ADVICE

Embrace the concept. Unions keep balance to a system that can be set off kilter if not managed. So many people become put off by the fact that they (as the boss) cannot just make decisions. They view the union as a stop sign to progress. However, this is the system in which we work. To constantly knock the union or look for ways around it creates the stoppages. Even the president has checks and balances. Why should we assume greater autonomy than the most powerful office in the world?

Remember the meeting before the meeting. The wise principal, when he or she has to make a controversial decision, usually gives the union leadership a heads-up prior to the decision being implemented. Do you have to do this? Heck no. But rest assured, if the decision involves people who may disagree, they will be visiting the union leadership on their own. No surprise. By telling the union leadership, he or she will be best ready to address the meeting with the person in a calm and collected manner.

The union can be your eyes. As the principal of the building, you cannot be everywhere all the time. However, the face of the union extends to the entire building. When issues of equity are in question, do not be surprised if your union leadership may slip you a hint or two about a situation that needs your attention (e.g., a teacher not going to his or her duty). Remember, a union is built on the premise of justice and equity. They can be your greatest ally when one of their own is not holding up his or her part of the bargain.

Know the teachers' contract. Understanding the contract will assist you in the dos and don'ts of the job. Obviously, once you build the team, you may be able to ask a favor here and there, but knowing the contract language will provide you with the foresight into a given situation.

Quick Think

If the race has already started, there are only three ways to lead —
run faster, stop, or turn.

TWENTY

Too Much Good Can Be a Bad Thing

Do you use sugar in your coffee? How many packets do you use? One? Two? Three tops? For most of us, a packet or two of our choice of sugar creates that satisfactory taste we so desire in our morning Joe. I would venture to say that some of us would consider sugar to be a good thing? Now, maybe you do not believe that consuming sugar in and of itself is a healthy habit, but to make the java taste just right, placing some of that "goodness" into your cup is a necessary evil. (Besides, we can hit the gym later, right?)

Now, suppose instead of placing the usual two packets of sugar in your coffee, we placed twenty-two? How do you think that would taste?

Too often, people in leadership positions substitute quantity for quality. In our search for the "next great initiative," we dismantle the effectiveness of our system (and the people within) by insisting on *more* when we have failed to gauge the historical and current practices, the data, and the assessment structures. In places where outcomes are undefined, the concept of "more" becomes the norm, creating the "something will eventually stick" motto. Leadership by dart board!

More does not necessarily translate into better. More translates into more, additional, extra, and judgments must be made whether or not people can handle more volume efficiently and effectively. Let us review the following scenario to witness this concept in action.

Marco was an elementary principal who was looking to reduce the after-school club class size. Currently, he was running six clubs. Each club consisted of one teacher and approximately thirty students. At a recent PTO meeting, discussions started around the clubs and the need for more sections to assist with class size.

Marco, in wanting to "meet the needs of the community," went back to his staff to see if anyone could run a different club. No one volunteered. (People are busy; they have families, take classes, and sometimes have other jobs as well. In these situations, try not to judge your folks too harshly. In these times, it is not easy to always give more time.) In wanting to give an assumed better program to students by reducing the class size, he went outside his staff and found two community members (with clearances) who committed to assisting with this endeavor.

Marco and the PTO were thrilled that there were now eight sections running and that class size was now approximately twenty-two students. However, what they did not anticipate was the complaints from the children and their families who were "sitting" in the newly designed sections. To expedite the example, the two community members were not teachers, had no teaching experience, and basically sat back while the students tried to figure out how to design and run a movie club. Many of the families then started to request that their children were not getting the same experience, and therefore, should be moved into another class. *You get the point here. More was not necessarily better.*

Of course Marco could have done more homework to find people who could facilitate the club successfully, but the crux of the issue started at the inception of the premise that more sections would equal better results. But the initial premise was doomed from the onset of the philosophy—more teachers absolutely mean better results.

Again, without a solid plan for objectives, strategies, and action steps, leaders associate *more* or *different* with *better*. Since there is no right answer for best practice, we sometimes create the false premise that change is the only answer. When leaders substitute more without awaiting data results from the previous work, they generate panic and a sense of inconsistent leadership.

A skilled principal knows that teachers are bridges, in that they have the potential to transfer so much to our students; however, like bridges, they can only support so much as well. Being able to gauge the "break points" is an invaluable skill, and one that will serve the leader well in trying to build connections.

PRACTICAL ADVICE

Survey the staff. There is nothing more valuable than keeping the pathways to communication open. Talk to the people. Find out how they are doing. They will be able to let you know how it is going. Of course, you might have to weigh different people's opinions (the complainers will always tell you they are overworked); however, when you do come upon a trend, be sure to acknowledge it and address it if possible. Golden Rule!

Plan at least a year ahead. Now, maybe this is not possible the very first year of being a principal, but once you get your feet on the ground, it is imperative to be ahead of the curve. As you are involving people with the plan, be sure to publish these ideas to continuously guide folks on expectations, on-goings, and so forth. In addition, by having an established plan that everyone is following, not only will the work have a better chance of being accomplished, but also folks will see your leadership as organized and systematic.

What's the win? Remember to stay focused on what is important. Does the staff really have to fill out those ten-page checkout lists at the end of the year, or is there another, more efficient manner to have everyone account for their belongings? These critical questions will guide you in the discovery of what needs to happen versus how it is being accomplished. Identify the win and plan accordingly.

TWENTY-ONE

The Number Line of Change

Chase Mitchell, a middle school assistant principal, was in charge of the new computer conversion in his building. Having known for over a year that the district was going to switch platforms for grading, attendance, and so on, he had attended all training sessions and really had a feel for the system. His goal was to train a few folks as trainers, and then they would provide (turn-around) training for the staff in May. He figured April would be a good time to start training people. He invited the team leaders to a brief after-school meeting and planned to share the details with them. No big deal, right?

As fate would have it, instead of a quick meeting to "introduce" the change, he walked into an all-out assault on him and the district. This was "one more thing" coming down the pike without their input! As Chase tried to explain that this decision was made months ago and teachers were in fact involved in the process, the only affirmation he received was the "whatever" stares. Too much. Too fast. Chase had lost before he had ever begun.

Why do people have such a difficult time with change? Maybe the answer lies in our values. Our society appreciates control. Actually, we are reminded of it every day: speed limits, red lights, and crossing guards (and that is all before we even get to school). Perhaps the state of control brings with it a feeling of safety for us. Being safe is healthy; therefore, perhaps staying in control promotes good health. Maybe not the most logical progression here, but I think you get the point.

Change, for some people, represents a giving-up of control, which creates an unhealthy feeling. Many people can and do survive and thrive when presented with change; however, when a change comes too fast, it often creates an imbalance of control. In a sense, the speed of the change (along with the impact) can dictate the level of acceptance and/or resistance.

Chase's leaders were pushed into a scrambled state; having no fore-warning of this change, they were "blindsided." In not having the oppor-tunity to digest the concept of the change (it was April, too late in the year), they were not given the opportunity to process their needs and the needs of their colleagues—the same colleagues that they (the team lead-ers) would have to train and ultimately hear their complaints.

To be most successful, change should come as natural as the number seven going to number eight then nine. We call this the Number Line of Change. Just as Wiggins with *Understanding by Design*, being able to iden-tify the outcome (the change) and plotting action steps to attain it make all the difference when it comes to planning a succinct and successful transition. For example, let us look at the current situation.

$$1 \quad\quad 2 \quad\quad 3 \quad\quad 4 \quad\quad 5 \quad\quad 6 \quad\quad 7 \quad\quad 8^* \quad\quad 9$$

$$\longrightarrow$$

*Have all teachers utilizing the new technology

Figure 21.1.

If Chase had identified the change and plotted it to the number eight, he would have been reminded that there were several (seven to be exact) action steps that would need to be addressed prior to achieving a normal progression (seven to eight to nine). Instead, Chase went from one to eight instantaneously. In skipping numbers, he caused stress to the sys-tem (the people), and the system pushed back (complaints).

Have you ever got into your car, turned the engine on, and been startled by the radio blasting at full volume? Change is like the music on a car radio. You want the people to "want" to turn up the volume, not be so surprised (and scared) by it that they turn it immediately off. Finding the right song at the right volume is the key.

PRACTICAL ADVICE

Involve the team. Although the district had already done so, Chase should have started the process earlier and involved his team. Even though the decision to utilize a new platform had been made, the implementation plan could have been negotiated between the team. We work with highly intelligent people. Utilize their expertise.

Determine if the change can be delayed. Some changes are not afforded the luxury of time (e.g., a fire bell rings and everyone must exit). For a crisis situation, we cannot "go to committee," so to speak. For those times, have a pronounced plan and practice it. Identify the protocols and leadership rank for smooth transitions. In non-crisis times, take your time. Take your time.

Share the plan. Remember the meeting before the meeting. Not much more to say about that.

Teach others this simple plan. The Number Line of Change can be used in all sorts of situations. Explain to your folks that you follow a protocol for planning change. Show them the action steps. This will help you with the change, but also work to instill confidence in your staff in that there is a plan and a way to turn ideas into action.

TWENTY-TWO

Try It

A "Try It" is a curt, practical idea that a principal can use immediately. A "Try It" ranges from concise strategies for success with people to simple actions to take in situations.

TRY IT: OFFICE TEAM MEETING

Although it might be commonplace to meet with the leadership of the building (team leaders, department heads, etc.), it may not be so overt to plan with the office team. Think about it, the very center of your organization resides within this entity. These people are the front line to the public and the backbone of support for the staff. It makes sense to get everyone on the same page.

Plan your meeting once a week, preferably in the early part of it. Invite the secretaries, guidance department, head custodian, assistant principals, and your attendance people. Have everyone review their weekly calendars and goals for the week. Ensure big event planning or special on-goings for the week. Likewise, this meeting provides a great opportunity for long-term planning as well. Consider this your production meeting before the "show" actually starts.

Once you finish the meeting agenda, excuse and thank the secretaries and custodians. Now you can have a guidance meeting with the principals. This is a great way to go over schedule-change requests or get the latest update on a family. Once that part is concluded, excuse and thank the guidance folks and meet as principals.

Championship teams are built based on an exceptional game plan. Make sure yours is worthy of a championship by holding office team meetings regularly.

TRY IT: POST THE BUDGET

I do not know what I would do without online banking. How about you? I just have that need to know what is going on with the account. Whether I am looking to pay bills or just figuring out next week's plan, I love the fact that the numbers are literally a few clicks away. Peace of mind.

Some would say that power is derived from having control over information and resources. If you believe this tenet to be true (or even somewhat true), posting the school's budget might be a wonderful way to empower your staff.

Most schools utilize some sort of building-based budgeting protocol. Whether you split the resources between departments or teams, the process of the budget usually involves soliciting opinions. There is tremendous power that comes when we share the financial goals of the building with everyone to build trust and understanding. Recall the online banking opening.

Do realize that you, as the principal, may have to justify more actions to the staff? But what is wrong with that? Offering the opportunity to know may just save you more work on different ends. It is up to you, but having learned from experience, posting the budget tells the staff we are in this together. Peace of mind.

TRY IT: PLAY HOME GAMES

Ask the opponents of the Green Bay Packers if they enjoy getting ready to play a game on the frozen tundra of Lambeau field or if visiting teams appreciate doing battle with the Boston Celtics at the Garden? Probably not! Home-field advantage has its rewards.

If you are going to work in a school, you have to learn to deal with emotion. From the students and parents to the teachers and counselors, dealing with children brings out the best and worst in us. People can be ecstatic about certain situations and quite the opposite about others. In those times, try to play home games.

Home games in schools are situations that are generated by us. Meetings, phone calls, and so forth become home games when we set the appointment and guide the agenda. For example, if a parent calls fuming about an issue, do not take the call until you have gathered all of the facts about the situation. Once you have the information, call the parent back. (Try to call parents at their work because they are less likely to behave poorly there. Sly but true.)

Home breeds familiarity. Do not allow yourself to get caught off guard. No surprises! Remind the staff to let you know when something is brewing, even if it is small potatoes right now. As the Packers at Lambeau, when we play a home game, the outcomes are more fortunate. I would love to see someone do a "Lambeau Leap" after a great parent conference. Wouldn't you?

TRY IT: THE RED FOLDER

Have you ever noticed that whenever you get really busy, that is when everyone wants to talk? It never fails. You are headed to an observation and someone wants to stop you in the hallway for a "quick second." Inevitably, there was nothing quick about that second or the one after that! Even when we try to politely tell the person we are busy, we find ourselves still spending precious minutes trying to leave. Late again.

Part of our job requires us to rank circumstances based on need. Emergencies go to the top, chit-chat sessions below. No one wants to be told that his or her priority is not yours, but that is often the case in leadership. How can we communicate in a compassionate way, but still get to where we need to go?

At the next faculty meeting, talk to the staff. Tell them that there are going to be times when you are *en route* to address a concern. Tell them you are going to carry a red folder. The red folder symbolizes concern for their issue, but at the present time, you need to address another. Oftentimes we forget who we see in the hallway because our brains are focused on the original issue; therefore, the red folder should also direct the hallway person to send you a quick email to set up a time to chat.

Admittedly, this type of tool can appear to be cold-hearted if not explained with kindred spirit. When addressing the staff, be honest, be polite, and as Obi-Wan would often say, "Use the folder, Luke."

TRY IT: FEED THE TEAM

If you are tired at the end of the day, that is a good thing. Chances are, you busted your hump throughout the periods and now have that sense of accomplishment that comes with *gratifying* fatigue. Now, you get to "celebrate" that weariness by having a faculty meeting. Yippee.

I know. I know. I should not knock faculty meetings. And every time I do, I get some suit snarling at me that we negotiated "long and hard to get that time." I realize that and value the efforts. I really do. But working with children is exhausting. And just as principals get tired, so does the staff.

If you are having an after-school meeting, nothing says "I appreciate you" more than a little nosh. Pretzels, apples, even water ice provides a bit of nourishment after a long day, but it also conveys your concern for their well-being. It is almost comical, grown people dragging themselves into the library with sour stances only to perk up when they notice a box of popsicles. The entire atmosphere of the meeting changes, as do our demeanors. What was once going to be a sullen sit-session is now a lively gathering.

Couple this idea with a few "try it" professional-development ideas, and you have got yourself a winner. Breakfast, lunch, or snacks, feeding the team works on so many levels.

"The belly rules the mind" (Spanish proverb).

TRY IT: SAFETY WALKS

In response to school violence, we were required to complete two safety walks a day (of the perimeter of the building). At first, we were a bit put off by the idea. Again, we are all busy and to chart these walks seemed contrived at best. In knowing I would be lambasted for refusing, I agreed with reservation. (Please note I was already securing the building periodically, and I just felt that charting the results was excessive.)

On the first walk, I noticed that the gym doors were propped open (a no-no in schools). I quickly chatted with the staff. We came to an amicable resolution (i.e., shut the doors and bring your key), and I forged ahead. Admittedly, I thought to myself, "Glad I saw that."

Once I got into a rhythm, I tended to look forward to the jaunts. Not only did it give me a chance to "clear my head," but it also was very beneficial in securing the building and documenting what I had addressed (just in case I had to chat with folks about propping the doors again). Likewise, the students would comment (when asked) that they felt safer knowing that we were out and about. Plus, our increased visibility builds cache with the staff too.

Got a pedometer?

TRY IT: SEND MINUTES

Baxter Berks was an assistant principal at one of our high schools. We would go to meetings, and I would always see him with his marble copybook taking copious notes. (Yes, this was before the days of laptops. We are old!)

To see him take these notes was like watching Tolstoy himself authoring a section of the *War and Peace* manuscript. His attention to detail was amazing. And the penmanship was impeccable. One day, my friends and I decided to rib him a bit about his "little black book." "Taking down a few phone numbers, Berksie," one of us questioned as the others chuckled.

Now Baxter had this wry smile that lets you know you are on his time. He glared at us fools and stated simply, "When I send out the minutes, I want to be accurate." In not wanting to seem like complete blockheads, we scrambled for some paper and proceeded to take notes with the hopes of relaying the information to our staff.

It had never occurred to me to send out minutes before, but the concept is so critical. People want to be "in the know." To facilitate genuine dialogue, it is our responsibility to facilitate the correct information to the masses. Nothing sets the record straight like well-written, straightforward minutes. Send them! Send them! Send them!

P.S. Baxter is now a superintendent in a neighboring school district and a close friend. And yes, he still takes notes in his little black books.

TRY IT: THE TALK OUT

When people are very upset about a given situation, most times, they will want to be heard. In trying to be responsive to their needs, administrators try to "fix" the problem without first allowing the person to totally explain the situation.

One of the best practices we can employ is to be an active listener. Instead of trying to give input, allow the person to talk out. Take an interested position; take notes. And really try to hear what is being said. This way, you allow the person to exhaust the emotion involved with a dicey situation.

I do admit when a person is attacking the school, the staff, or you personally, it is difficult to keep your cool. However, as stated time and time again, always be professional. Stay focused on the end game—solving the situation to make it better for the student, staff members, or family. We are a people business. As Patrick Swayze used to say, "Be nice."

TRY IT: PEOPLE, THEN THINGS

One time I heard a teacher state, "You can't speak up to the administration." As I thought about this statement, I have to admit I believed it to be true. In fact, I cannot think of any job where it is permissible to "speak up" to your boss. It was not until many years later that I realized what this person was trying to communicate. In this instance, the teacher who made the original statement was upset because there was no forum to communicate with her administrator.

Often too busy to touch base with one another, little problems between the teacher and principal became bigger and started to erode the positive culture that both the teacher and principal desired. Needless to say, that principal was me, and I was screwing it up big time.

When I was a boy, I had broken a locket very valuable to my mother. As I sat on the couch with the pieces of the locket in my hand, my mother could tell something was wrong. As the tears began, I will never forget what my mom said to me. With the compassion and patience that only a mother can have, she said, "Things can be replaced. People can't." As I reflect back on these words, I realize the enormous influence that this little statement has had on my life.

Things can be replaced. People can't.

Most times, when we lose in the relationship arena, we do so because we have placed a higher value on things than on people. With that being said, do your best to put the people first when dealing with situations. That's the win-win!

TRY IT: COME CLOSER

Suppose you were having conversation with an atheist and a zealot and each was trying to convince you to convert to their line of thinking. What methodology do you believe each would use to gain your favor?

Most times, when people are trying to establish a stance, they use facts and opinions to strengthen their position and also diminish their opponents. However, the majority of people sit right in the middle when it comes to issues between extremes. The more opposites try to prove their points (and move away from each other) the more difficult it is for the middle to move toward either of them.

When trying to "convince" others, perhaps the greatest play we can make is to move closer to what our adversary believes. In starting with the idea of compromise, we forgo the typical boasting that is associated with positioning. Remember, what's the win? Look for ways to accomplish the goal without compromising the relationship.

It is also wise to understand that when you do move to an extreme, you may be there by yourself. In being a principal and having the tasks of allocating resources in a limited environment, you will get more bees with honey for everyone rather than supplying all to a special-interest group. And when you have to support a special-interest group over the majority, be sure to define your rationale rather than assuming understanding as an outcome of your action. Remember, they don't call it "rock and rock."

TRY IT: HAVE A WITNESS

Have you even been caught in the middle of a "he said, she said" hullabaloo? If you were, chances are it took substantial time out of your day only to have your justifications rendered null and void by the other person's reasons. And no matter how accurate you take and present your notes, the standard "that's your opinion" will always be a viable option to refute your points.

There are going to be times in this job when people are going to disagree with your account of a specific event. *Nothing justifies the facts more than a witness's account.*

In heading into dismissal hearings, discipline reviews, parent meetings, challenging IEPs, and so on, make it part of your practice to have a witness in these types of situations.

The witness can be another principal, your administrative assistant, a counselor, or someone else not directly involved in the situation. Ask this person to take notes and be a great listener. This way, if the time ever comes to review the situation, this person will be able to present a non-biased interpretation of the event. Plus, the witness can also serve as a protection for the other person as well. (Not that you would do anything wrong, but it never hurts to offer support for all.)

This may seem like a no brainer, and in fact, it is! Have a witness.

TRY IT: BUILDING PRIDE USING OTHER MEDIUMS

Do you know anyone that goes to work without brushing their teeth, combing their hair, and the like? Okay. One might be late on occasion and skip the shower or plan ahead and shower the night before. However, people who continuously fail in these areas usually get noticed, and not in a nice manner, I might add.

As leaders, we do have to realize that our appearance matters. In knowing this, how come so many buildings look so darn dirty? Now, we are not here to bash the custodial team or look to point fingers at central maintenance. Obviously, these folks need to perform well in their areas to assist us with ours.

What we are referring to is the "personality" of our buildings, whether new construction or an aged building. As the educational leaders, we can add that "something special" to a building by incorporating the mission into the design. Murals, music, catching quotes, team-recognition hallways, and so on, are all excellent ways to bring the building to life.

Our buildings, as noted by OWP/P Architects, VS Furniture, and Bruce Mau Design in *The Third Teacher: 79 Ways You Can Use Design to Transform Teaching and Learning*, demonstrate just how the physical environment can impact the culture. Keep these ideas in mind the next time you walk through the school. You know what it is now, but what can it be . . . and why!

TRY IT: PUTTING PEOPLE'S PASSION INTO ACTION

We all have passions outside of our regular school life. Perhaps you are a swimmer or maybe enjoy a nice game of bridge. Whatever your fancy, there are specific reasons why people immerse themselves into their areas of interest. "Better find a job you love to do or else life can get pretty glum." (Not even sure if we still use the term *glum*, but you get the point.) People who enjoy their work seem to enjoy life more often.

If the later statement could be true, it's a wonder why we do not try to marry our passion to our professions. Now, understand that if you have a group of teachers that love to jog, you can't just pull a treadmill into their classrooms and think that works.

However, perhaps you can help them start a jogging club, or maybe you can encourage them to select a few stories about jogging for their next literature circle. Or maybe you can buy that treadmill and allow people to use it after school. The point is, when leaders take the time to get to know their staff and their passions, they have a better chance to build and sustain a positive environment.

One school I visited called these committees *action teams*. They were completely voluntary and were focused on building a positive environment. They really seemed to work well! Try it out. See what your folks like and start to run (or jog) with those ideas.

TWENTY-THREE
Don't Try It

A "Don't Try It" is the opposite of a Try It. A "Don't Try It" is decision that should not be made by educational leaders, for it often causes dissatisfaction with staff, students, families, and ultimately, one's self.

DON'T TRY IT: JOKES IN POWER

Just as there are ideas to try, there are also some you should avoid at all costs. One such suggestion has to do with "trying" to be funny. We all know the type—the boss that loves to dig his fellow employees—meant as "good clean fun," the smiling sophisticate saunters up to the next potential target. Maybe he is uncomfortable in social situations. Maybe he is looking for acceptance. Maybe he is just an ass!

Whatever the rationale for this person, one thing is certain—he is going to crack a joke. And when he does, it's not going to be funny. Why? Because inevitably, someone is going to be hurt by his comments, and there isn't a darn thing the employee can do about it. (Of course, if someone is being harassed, he or she can contact Human Resources. But an occasional pun from the boss hardly elicits an action worthy of notice.)

Statements like "I'd just fire you" or "Let's weigh our wallets" are not funny. They are subtle (and not so subtle) reminders. They serve to ascend the boss's role by diminishing the employee. These "comical" witticisms erode the fabric of a positive climate, leading to an all-out assault on the culture.

Jokes in power are not jokes; they are reminders of who is in charge.

Remember when mom used to say if you don't have something nice to say. . . . Well, take that little nugget and carry it all the way up the administrative ladder. Avoid the mixture of humor and rank, as the combination is as lethal as carbon monoxide and a silent killer of morale as well.

DON'T TRY IT: REWARDING ONE

During one of my undergraduate classes, my professor used the "Apple" experiment to make a great point. To make a long story longer, she used to give a team midterm. At the start of the next class, she would present two groups (out of six) with apples and state how proud she was of their efforts. Without mentioning scores (or even handing back the tests), she would proceed with class as normal.

As break would conclude, she would pass out the assessments. Inevitably, the class would soon figure out that the two lauded groups had similar scores to the entire class. Without fail, she would sit and wait for someone to ask, "Why did they get an apple and we did not?" And with that, she would start the lesson on motivation. (Nice job, Dr. M.)

Sparing you a dissertation on motivational research, know that people can sometimes be fragile (or "fra geel lee" if you are Darren McGavin fan) in our business. Rarely are individuals motivated by the rewards of others. Nominating one staff member for Teacher of the Year sends myriads of others into the hallway questioning their worth.

I am not saying that timely praise is unhealthy. Large group accomplishments can and should be shared as a team. However, for individual triumphs, chat with the person in private. Many a principal has had the best of intentions when it comes to praising his or her staff only to witness the floor crumble beneath their feet. Think fruit: if you are going to give out apples, you had better buy a bushel.

DON'T TRY IT: BEING THE PRINCIPAL

I know an administrator who is probably the nicest human being you will ever meet. He is kind, supportive, and truly a child advocate. Unfortunately, his greatest asset (wanting people to get along) is also his greatest fault.

A principal has the responsibility of keeping balance to the system. In a sense, we have to ensure that the rights of the individuals and the rights of the collective are in harmony. In juggling this critical act, sometimes we will affirm people's needs, and sometimes we will need to say "no."

If you are the type of person that has a hard time with people being annoyed with you, you might want to work on this trait prior to taking the job. Just as a parent cannot allow a child to eat whatever the child wants prior to bedtime, there will be times when you are going to have to "parent" different situations with your staff. We cannot allow ourselves to be nervous addressing situations for fear of upsetting the apple cart.

In looking for the win-win situation, one does not have to acquiesce to garner favor with others.

Leadership by bartering only serves to build false expectations.

Just as a parent who bribes a child to go to bed with candy can create a covetous little one, so too can we create the illusion of compliance when we substitute an external motivation (in this case, a false rationale for action) for what should be internal (wanting to do it because it is right or even because we have to do so). Too much good can sometimes be a bad thing. It's okay to say *no* and mean it.

DON'T TRY IT: THE GENERAL WARNING

We have all received one of these emails:

> Good morning everyone,
> It has come to my attention that several members of our staff are still arriving late to school. As stated in last month's faculty meeting, our workday starts at *7:30 a.m.* We cannot continue to arrive late to school, as this practice is both violating the contract and also causing a morale problem for those who arrive on time!!!! Thank you for your compliance.
> Mr. Thomas Morris

How do you feel reading this email? Now imagine how your staff feels. Tom had addressed the issue in a previous faculty meeting and instead of having the personal conversation (and more difficult one), he opted to again use a general warning. Come on, Tom!

Look . . . everyone knows when someone is coming in late, leaving early, skipping their duty, and so on. Too often, administrators veil behind the general warnings when best practice would be to put the laptop down and stand in the hallway at 7:25 a.m. And if someone is late, let them know. Define the expectations with respect, dignity, and a smidgen of firmness.

As stated before, principals need to keep the balance. This tenet will also ask us to administer between the people that do what they are supposed to do and those that do not. Please, please, please do not take the easy way out. Better to be a little uncomfortable now than to try and fix a culture that is stained by our inability to do the tough work.

DON'T TRY IT: CHANGING DECISIONS ON
THE ASSISTANTS' ACTIONS

Martha was an excellent assistant principal. She worked diligently on whatever project that was put in front of her. She was especially sound at speaking to students about their mistakes (discipline issues).

On one particular occasion, Vincent, the principal, got wind of a student-discipline issue that Martha had processed. It seems that the student's father knew the principal and actually called him at his home to inquire about the amount of days that his son received for a suspension. Vincent, without consulting Martha, decided to overturn the suspension and allowed the student to attend classes in the morning.

When Martha arrived at school, she was surprised to see the boy in school. When she politely questioned him, he stated that his dad "made a deal" with the principal. Martha immediately spoke to Vincent about the situation and was "politely" excused, as was his prerogative as the principal to make a change, along with the fact that this child "came from a good family." Martha returned to her office, a little wiser than before about her boss and his belief system.

Do you have the right, as the principal, to change the discipline? Yes. Should you? Not without a conversation with your administrative team. Without the discussion, all we have done is create mistrust between ourselves and the team while also telling the rest of the school that the team really doesn't have any power. When we undercut a member of the team, the entire team suffers. Needless to say, Martha no longer works with Vincent.

DON'T TRY IT: THE ADMINISTRATIVE APOLOGIST

When we make a mistake, it is certainly par for the course to apologize. Many a person has gained respect and admiration for admitting fault; however, there are those that seem to apologize for everything as a substitute for being direct. "I am sorry, but I have a coverage for you. Sorry, but I need you to take this remedial class. I am so sorry about asking you to come to the IEP meeting."

As a principal, we do not have to be "sorry" for items that are required of us (and others) to do our job. Perhaps this practice goes back to our wanting to be liked. Or maybe we truly do feel bad when we have to delegate work to others. Whatever the case, saying we are sorry for a non-fault communicates to the other person that something must be wrong with the given situation. "Why would the principal be sorry for asking me to do a coverage unless it was a really tough class?" In addition, being sorry now diminishes the true sincerity of the apology when we really mean it.

We would never want to portray the image of being brash; however, we also would not want to give the impression of being soft either. When delegating assignments, act with respect, but forgo the need to apologize.

"If everyone is happy, something might be a brewin'" (anonymous).

DON'T TRY IT: QUITE HONESTLY

When I was finished presenting at my first board meeting, my superintendent called me to come to his office. He asked me to watch the tape of the board meeting and comment on my performance. (In my district, we film the board meetings and project live to the public.)

When I was finished viewing the tape, I went back to him and asked what was up. "How do you think you did?" he asked. I remember telling him I thought I did a pretty good job, but still had a few items to work on. At that moment, he said, "Quite honestly."

Since I wasn't sure what he meant by that, I asked him to explain. He then directed me back to the tape. I had not even noticed it, but I had said "quite honestly" about 37 million times. Yikes!

When I went back to him, he explained that we (as administrators) are in a position that must portray trust. When we use starters like "quite honestly," we are telling the people that perhaps we have not been honest with the prior conversations.

He had realized that I was not trying to mislead anyone. It was a nervous reaction that was being substituted as a speech pattern. Sometimes, we develop these "helpers" to tell the listener when we are about to disagree with them or perhaps present something controversial. As principals, we need to examine our speech patterns to hear what we are "saying" to people (whether we mean it or not).

Look for ways to communicate your thoughts without using the verbal crutches.

DON'T TRY IT: HINTING AT CONFIDENTIAL MATTERS

It is funny how often we learn something in grade school and it becomes a life lesson. Remember that childhood chant, "I know something, but I won't tell." Remember what your teacher would say when someone was singing it? Chances are, it was not a pleasurable response. But why?

When people hint to confidential matters, they create a sense of power for themselves (we know something) while also creating a feeling of helplessness for the listener (but I won't tell). Most times, the information (critical or not) is presented as an imperative—serving to heighten anxiety and provide a power imbalance (I *won't* tell).

People in positions of power (having information) play this little game all the time. Whether purposeful ("I wish I could tell you about the discipline situation") or not ("My day is crazy busy; got this huge discipline issue to handle"), these types of comments create an imbalance of the haves and have nots.

If you are working on something you know you cannot talk about, then don't talk about it. Hinting to it without a definable explanation creates ill feelings. Likewise, when someone asks us how our day is going, we may be "very busy," but to imply that we are busier than the people around us again produces a divide in the team. "My day is pretty hectic, as I am sure yours is teaching students how to read." Simple tags to the original line may serve to foster a greater sense of togetherness.

DON'T TRY IT: THE "AFTER-CONFERENCE" NEW INITIATIVE

Has your principal ever gone to a conference and returned the next day looking to change the entire educational system starting with your school? It's unreal. They spend fifty minutes with the next "guru" and think they have found the Holy Grail of education. What's worse is they rush back to their school and initiate all kinds of stress and anxiety on their colleagues. It's just wrong!

We, as educational leaders, must show support and confidence in our team and their work. To completely want to change the course based on a conference shows our lack of vision and commitment to it. Don't get me wrong. Conferences can be a tremendous source of information and idea sharing; yet to take any isolated idea and redirect the course of your school based on it is ill advised.

When looking at topics for conferences, be sure to plan ahead. Look to see how the conference may fit into the vision and mission of the district. Select sessions where people would expect you to bring back information. Now, if you happen to attend sessions that peak your interest to think differently, that is awesome! But do not run back to school and plan a revolution.

At first, keep the idea to yourself. Research and review the data. Think about the pros and cons. Then start to share this idea with your key people (the meeting before the meeting). Maybe they will see something you have not. Find a way to make it their idea and not yours.

Negotiate in times of peace.

DON'T TRY IT: CALLING A MEETING WITHOUT A TOPIC

Has this ever happened to you: You get a message from your boss, who wants to see you right away . . . only there is no topic assigned to the message? Talk about panic city. You wrack your brain trying to think about all of the issues you have dealt with in the last week. Anxiety gets the better of you, and when you finally meet, the topic is never as grand as what you assumed.

I would like to consider that your boss was just in a hurry and did not have time to give the details about the discussion topic. However, experience has demonstrated that occasionally, these folks like being "in charge" of our time.

When you call your next meeting, forego the power trip and be sure to give a topic with the message. Even if it is not urgent (math books two years out), your colleagues will appreciate the gesture. And be sure to let them know that nothing is wrong by saying, "Nothing bad." Conversely, when there is something critical to discuss, you can always say, "Have Mr. So and So give me a call."

I understand there are going to be times when you do not want the person taking the message to know everything you are discussing. Yet I still believe that a simple topic and curt phone call go a long way in maintaining positive morale and a great working relationship.

TWENTY-FOUR

Case Studies

The following are situations that connect to each chapter. They are designed to spur conversation and look to examine the key points of each chapter. Oftentimes, the case study is best when used prior to reading the chapter.

CHAPTER 1
MARTIAL ARTS MENTALITY

George Brody, the principal of Ford High School, was having a conversation with his colleagues during a recent meeting. When asked how the year was coming along, he replied, "My school is having a fantastic year! My staff is really working hard to attain all district and school-based goals, and the scores resemble a high commitment toward student achievement. In addition, I had an idea of how to use part of homeroom as a tutoring session for our struggling students. My assistant principals are working on the details as we speak. Other than that, it is business as usual at FHS."

Notice anything about this response? Can you draw any loose conclusions about Principal Brody? Would you revise this reply? If so, how?

CHAPTER 2
TRY IT: MAKING CHANGE MORE EFFECTIVE

Please read this letter sent from Dr. Melissa Klen, an elementary principal, who was writing to her staff concerning the opening day of school:

Greetings Everyone,

Can you believe that the start of the school year is upon us! I certainly hope that you and your family are enjoying a peaceful and fulfilling summer. It has been a very busy summer for Trendy Elementary School. But one I would not trade for the world!

Please note the official start date is August 31 at 8:30 a.m. at Trendy. On this day, we will be joined by Dr. Joyce Bloss, from Bloss and Associates. She will be providing you with Working Reading Strategies. The hope would be for implementation of these strategies starting on our first RTI rotation in September. Dr. Bloss specializes in struggling readers and will be able to provide you with valuable tools for your toolbox.

We are also lucky to have Mr. Ken Mann on September 1 to assist you in learning new ways to teach problem-solving in math and science. You might remember Ken as a "Teacher to Watch" from Gentry School District. I worked with Ken for many years and find him to be an excellent resource for teachers who may not be as versed in teaching math and science, as elementary folks can sometimes tend to be.

I have also planned out the year's professional-development schedule, and you will be receiving that (along with a few other items) on opening day.

For now, I wish you a happy and safe rest of the summer. Looking forward to seeing you all very soon.

Sincerely,
Dr. Melissa Klen

What do you notice about this letter with regards to the professional-development plan? What assumptions are being made? How could you revise this letter? This process?

CHAPTER 3
THE MEETING BEFORE THE MEETING

Carol Phelps, the principal of River Springs Middle School, was meeting with her team leaders about the new district technology plan. As she was unveiling the plan, she was very disappointed in the reactions of the team. Jim, a long-time team leader and usually someone Carol could rely on, was being extremely passive-aggressive. When Carol asked if there were any questions, Jim rolled his eyes and literally turned away in his chair.

"Is there a problem, Jim?" Carol questioned. Jim, in realizing Carol's displeasure, just shook his head and proceeded to sit in silence, as did the rest of the team. Upon completion, the meeting dispersed.

Carol, in being a conscientious person, could not understand what just happened. She sat in disbelief and wondered if this negative reaction to the plan, to her, or to both.

What were some factors that cause this meeting to go awry? What was the initial issue? Could it have been avoided? What could Carol do next time? What should she do now? What would you do?

CHAPTER 4
HOW MANY IS MANY

In being the principal of Deer Woods High School, you are confronted by three passionate band students who are reporting that everyone is upset by the new regulations for band events. Despite having a committee that developed the regulations (comprised of teachers, students, and administrators), the students believe they were "devalued" in the process.

They also believe that there is so much support for their position that this Saturday's competition will be boycotted, hence lowering the funding source for the band (ticket sales, refreshments—money allocated to buy new uniforms) and placing a great deal of stress on the already stressed band director (students not showing up for the competition).

In mentioning this situation to one of the assistant principals, she comments that a boycott could cause "terrible press for the school," as this competition involves twenty other schools from surrounding districts.

It is Tuesday. The event takes place Saturday. What's your game plan?

118 *Chapter 24*

CHAPTER 5
THAT'S WHY YOU MAKE THE BIG BUCKS!

Dr. Daryl Wilson, principal of Jameson Middle School, was in a quandary. In need of tutors for the struggling student population, he could not find a single person to take the job. In being a principal for seven years in another district, he did not expect to hit this much resistance at Jameson, a school known for going "above and beyond" for students.

Daryl had mentioned the situation to one of his department heads. He joked if he could not find a volunteers, he might have to tutor the students himself. The response to his jest was, "This is a tough situation, Dr. Wilson. Guess that's why you make the big bucks."

Daryl politely chuckled, and the conversation ceased.

In reviewing this situation, what type of culture would you say exists at Jameson Middle School? What could Daryl do to find tutors? Is tutoring the issue? What would you do?

CHAPTER 6
THE "HOW DOES THAT WORK?" MEETING

The principal of Devon Elementary school, Mrs. Joan Tyler, was a very busy woman. Having just concluded an intense budgeting cycle template, she was now working on her staffing matrix for the following year, which was due in two days.

Earlier, Joan had asked Ms. Webber, Joan's administrative assistant, to email the new budget totals to her department heads. As Ms. Webber left the office, Joan stated, "With the new state regulations, everything is becoming more difficult to manage." Ms. Webber agreed.

About twenty minutes later, Ms. Webber returned to Joan's office upset. "I am getting several emails from the department heads, and now from the staff, about the changes in budget allocations. I am not sure how to respond."

If you were Joan, what would you do? What could you have done prior to this?

CHAPTER 7
EMBRACE THE ANTITHESIS

Mr. Myles Graves was an exact man. This being his third year as a high school principal, he was used to conflict and had a direct way of dealing with it. In this particular "brainstorming" session, several members of his leadership team were discussing what the future of the high school should be. Myles was known for strategic planning, and had always prided himself on being "organized for progress."

As the topic focused upon the purpose of school, one leader commented that he thought school should "serve to provide students with an exploration into possibilities." Within this frame of thinking, students would use school as a trial-and-error lab through which they could discover different pathways to assist with their future planning.

Upon hearing this comment, Myles retorted, "Exploration is nice, but would that raise your SAT scores or afford you the opportunity to attend an Ivy League School?" With that, the conversation shifted toward assessment and changes that needed to be made in the progress-monitoring process.

What is your opinion of the purpose of a high school? How should that fit into the building of a collective mission? How's Myles doing?

CHAPTER 8
COMMON THREADS: A METHODOLOGY FOR
INVESTIGATIONS IN SCHOOLS

A student has just entered your office and made an accusation that another student has been bullying her. Simultaneously, a second student enters and begins to retort the first's explanation, stating that she has text messages in which the first girl is the one who is doing the bullying.

As you begin to speak, your guidance counselor motions to you and explains that there are three other young ladies stating that girl number two is lying and that they had told Mr. Douglas, a seventh-grade teacher, about this bullying weeks ago, but he did not do a thing about it.

As the chief investigator of this situation, please plan out the steps you would take toward a resolution, including the method of investigating, the possible disciplinary actions, and the informing of all stakeholders involved.

CHAPTER 9
WHAT'S THE WIN?

As the principal, you are in the middle of a tense IEP meeting. The parent, along with her advocate, is demanding that the school provide services for a child that the data does not seem to support. As the meeting progresses, one of the regular education teachers disagrees with the suggestion made by the advocate. As he tries to respond, the advocate interrupts. The teacher quickly replies, "I was not finished talking. If you would wait until people finish, then maybe we could have an intelligent dialogue."

Knowing that you are only on page ten of a twenty-three-page document, what would you do? Please be sure to plan action steps that include from this point of the meeting until a potential conclusion. In your words, what's the win in this situation?

CHAPTER 10
YOU DON'T KNOW WHAT YOU DON'T KNOW

Pam Grundy was very upset. In being the principal of Scott High School, she was furious about a decision the Human Resources director had made concerning the discipline of a teacher. To make a long story short, this particular teacher made a crude remark to a student. Pam, in knowing that this was "not the first time" this teacher had done something like this, wanted the teacher to be suspended. However, Ms. Jeffers, the HR director, resolved the issue with a verbal reprimand.

When Pam finally calmed, she spoke to Ms. Jeffers, who proceeded to tell her that there were "extenuating circumstances" that she could not discuss with Pam, and that Pam was going to have to "trust" her decision in being right.

If you were Pam, how would you react to this answer? What would be your next move? Can you be satisfied in "not knowing" all of the details?

CHAPTER 11
THE NEW COMPETITION

You are the principal of Grants Middle School, and your sixth-grade teachers are broken into teams (five teachers per team, three teams total). On this particular day, the blue team leader shares with you that his team is "very upset" by the red team. It appears that the red team has planned a field trip to a famous museum and has not included the other two teams.

No sooner does the blue team leader exit your office then the White team leader appears and states that his team is also upset (but not with the red team). His team is upset with the blue team for purchasing team shirts for the teachers for a special spirit day they are planning to have next Friday. The white team feels like they will "look bad" to their students for not having the same level of school spirit.

In being the principal, how will you handle these situations? Be sure to address the idea of competition. Is competition healthy? Should teams be "exact" to one another? It is up to you.

CHAPTER 12
THE FIVES TEST

As the principal of Shining Elementary School, you have had a great ten-year run. Scores are high, your staff is exceptional, and your community is satisfied with your work and the outcomes for their children. One day, your boss approaches you about possibly being the next principal of the district's middle school. Unfortunately, the middle school is not performing as well as Shining. Morale is down, as well as the achievement scores. In fact, you have heard people refer to the middle school as the "great abyss" of the district. Your boss assures you that she will not "force" you to go, but would like you to consider it.

Will you go? Will you stay? What are the ramifications of each? What decision-making method will you utilize to make this decision?

CHAPTER 13
ON SAVING FACE

Helen Jones, a seventh-grade math teacher, had just finished telling you that another teacher on the staff was checking his email and taking personal phone calls during class. Helen, in being a bit nervous to "go against" another staff member, requested explicitly to not be named as the source. You agreed.

In a meeting with this other teacher and his union representative, you are questioned about the origin of these accusations. In not wanting to reveal the source, you deny answering that question. At this point, the union representative states that the investigation cannot continue, as without knowing the source, there is no way for this teacher to defend the accusations.

Both the union representative and the teacher begin to leave your office.

What do you do? What should you have done prior to this point?

CHAPTER 14
DON'T BITE THE BOSS

At a recent principals meeting, your colleagues were complaining about a new initiative that your assistant superintendent was trying to implement. The principals were upset because you all were not given a chance to give your opinion on the topic (which seems to be her way). As you sit at the meeting, you learn that the other principals are going to "quietly" boycott the new initiative by just politely agreeing with the assistant superintendent, but not following through on any of the work.

Two days later, the assistant superintendent is visiting your building and asks how everything is going.

Do you tell her about the plan? What are the costs/benefits of your actions? What if she directly asked you if people were complaining about this initiative?

CHAPTER 15
THE BUY IN IS OUT

Bonnie Roads, the principal of Loomis Elementary School, decided that her school needed a spring fair. In speaking with the PTO, she assured her constituents that the teachers "would be fine" once she got them to buy into the concept. The PTO parents were so excited that they posted the date on Facebook prior to ending the meeting.

Is there anything wrong with this line of thinking? What is the message that you are sending to the staff?

CHAPTER 16
ROCK AND ROLL

Mrs. Sanders, a good-hearted teacher, has a problem. Johnny Wiseman was late to her homeroom again. In fact, this is the third time this week he has been late. As the assistant principal, Mrs. Sanders has written a referral and is asking you to discipline him because "if we allow Johnny to be late, what kind of message are we sending to the other students?"

Mr. Bell, the school guidance counselor, overhears this conversation. Afterward, he feels compelled to inform you that Johnny's father walked out on the family last month. In fact, he believes that since Johnny's mother has to work two jobs now, Johnny has had to make sure that his sisters get on the bus to attend elementary school, a possible reason for his morning lateness. In overhearing about the referral for Johnny, he implores you not to discipline him.

When you check his attendance record from the previous year, you do notice that Johnny, although not a discipline problem, has been late before. In fact, one could make an argument that he has a lateness problem.

Knowing that the discipline policy calls for a two-day internal suspension and a citation for truancy, which could be a $100 fine, what will you do with Johnny? Be sure to address all possible stakeholders in your response.

CHAPTER 17
MY MIRACLE

Mrs. Knowles, a parent of Michael (an eighth-grade student with autism), sits in front of you with tears in her eyes. Her son does not have any friends, and she is asking you for help. Although you have tried to assist with this situation before, Michael can sometimes demonstrate antisocial behavior.

Would you help? Is it your responsibility to ensure kids have friends? If so, what would be your plan to assist? Which stakeholders would you involve? What if Michael was prone to violent outbursts? Would that change your perspective? Should it change his mother's?

CHAPTER 18
THEY HAVE FORGOTTEN WHERE THEY ARE FROM

A group of teachers were gathered at their cars after a recent faculty meeting. It appears that their principal, once again, had decided that they were going to take a new approach to team time. Instead of progress-monitoring a group of selected students, her decision was to progress-monitor everyone because "if it is good for some kids, then it is good for everyone."

If you were a teacher on this staff, what would be your initial reaction? Talk about the ramifications of such a philosophy and decision? Would you tell the principal? How would you respond as the principal?

CHAPTER 19
THE UNION WITH THE UNION

It is the practice in most school districts that when a teacher needs to be spoken to, he or she is permitted to bring a union representative to the meeting. In knowing that the union representative does not need to be given permission to speak at these meetings, will you allow the union representative to speak?

What are the pros and cons of this decision?

CHAPTER 20
TOO MUCH GOOD CAN BE A BAD THING

At a recent technology meeting at the district office, Ms. Nash, the technology coordinator for your district, has offered two full sets of computers (sixty total computers/not laptops) to any school that wishes to have them, as a vender had recently given a two-for-one deal to a consortium.

In being the principal of an elementary school at enrollment capacity, do you take the computers? What are the ramifications of your decision? Who wins? Who loses?

CHAPTER 21
THE NUMBER LINE OF CHANGE

Marcia Downs, a high school principal, sure has her work cut out for her. In trying to increase rigor for student achievement, Marcia has revised the student schedule. Obviously, in revising the student schedule, many of the teacher schedules will also change as well. In a meeting with her union leader, Marcia was questioning why so many people were upset by these changes. "No one flinched when I changed the two-hour-delay schedule that did not work (people were losing their prep time). Why are they so upset at this change?"

If you were the union representative, how would you respond? Even though it is the prerogative of Marcia to change a schedule, what advice could you give her for future changes?

Situations

The following pages present circumstances that need to be analyzed by you, the principal of your building. Take some time and work through the critical points by utilizing some of the lessons you have garnered from this text.

You arrive back at your building from a morning in-service at the start of period four. Please rank and justify your rankings as to how you would handle these situations/referrals/notes. *You will only have four minutes to complete this timed assignment.

Guidance Counselor: "There is a student waiting to see you. She thinks Tom Grodes may have drugs on him, but she is not sure. What do you want to do?"

Secretary: "Your Superintendent called and needs to speak with you immediately. Shall I put her through?"

Mrs. White: "There is a mistake with the PSSA testing schedule for next Thursday's test. Now what?"

Mr. Task: "There is a blue car in the parking lot with the lights on."

Police: "Someone just dialed 911. You will need to meet with Officer Tyler."

NOW HIRING

As a member of the hiring committee, it is your responsibility to select staff. Your Human Resources director has provided you with three finalists for a vacant English position in your high school. Both the job description and a description of the finalist are below. Understanding that "you can only gather so much from a description, please rank the candidates in the order that you would hire them. Be sure to include your reasoning. What factors assisted you with this decision? (Assume that all applicants have similar educational backgrounds that would qualify them for the position.)

Ninth-Grade Honors English Opening, Mayfield Suburban High School

Applicants must have a firm grasp of literature as it applies to Shakespearean dramas. Likewise, applicants must possess superior skills in grammar, vocabulary, medieval poetry, and the writing process. Applicants must also be student-centered, highly motivated team players who will go the extra mile for their students. In addition, applicants that can offer leadership outside the classroom will be considered in high regard. This is a contracted position.

Applicant #1

This veteran teacher is returning to the classroom after a six-year stint as a stay-at-home mother. Previously, she was a department chair in her inner-city school district, where she taught twelfth-grade honors and academic classes. She has been an assistant drama director in the past, but would really prefer to try something new this time around. Although she has never taught ninth grade before, she "has a middle school child" at home and assumes basic similarities, which would make her qualified for the position. In addition, she is a community member and volunteers once a month at the local soup kitchens.

Applicant #2

This teacher is in her third year at a neighboring school. Currently, she is teaching ninth-grade English to academic and basic students. Her curriculum mirrors Mayfield's ninth-grade program with the exception of the Shakespearean dramas. Instead, their focus is on the novel, specifically *Great Expectations*. She is currently a varsity head soccer coach and her team was runner up in district's last season. Although she is happy in her position, she would like to move closer to home.

Applicant #3

This teacher is in his tenth year at your middle school. He is currently an eighth-grade English and reading teacher. He also has a degree in special education. He comes with high recommendations from his principals. In addition, he is known to be a great organizer. Currently, he serves on your district's strategic-planning committee. He has mentioned in his interview that although he has never formally taught honors sections, "English is English!" He was recommended for the Fellowship Award last year, an award given by his school to the teacher with the most compassion for children.

Please evaluate this letter of recommendation:
  October

Mrs. Joan Wayne
Assistant Principal
Cleary High School
Western, PA 19380

RE: Recommendation for Mr. Thomas Smallwood

To Whom It May Concern:
I am pleased to recommend Mr. Thomas Smallwood, an administrative intern at Clearly High School. Mr. Smallwood has fulfilled all of the duties of the internship at an appropriate level of competency. Whether it is completing the master schedule, assisting teachers with curricular and instructional needs, or coordinating our outdoor education program, Mr. Smallwood has completed all of the necessary preparation and planning to witness the achievement of each event.

Likewise, I feel compelled to discuss some of his philosophies concerning children. Mr. Smallwood prides himself on being student centered. His willingness to volunteer to coach football has definitely given him an interesting perspective on students in and outside of the classroom.

In closing, Mr. Smallwood certainly has made quite a memorable impression on the entire staff! Please feel free to call me if you wish to discuss Mr. Smallwood further at 813-367-8100.

Thank you for your support in this matter.

Mrs. Joan Wayne
Assistant Principal

What is Mrs. Wayne really saying in this recommendation? Should she have even written it?

Upon being named principal of Suburban School, please respond to the following five letters. What issues are surfacing? How will you address each?

Letter #1

Dear Principal,

As a dedicated teacher in Suburban School, I wish to fill you in on a few things that need to be brought up before "your stay" with us commences.

We are a staff that pride ourselves on professionalism and high expectations. We have weathered the tide of administrations that have come and gone; we have educated some of the finest minds in our great community. We respect our school and its core of values.

As you may know, coming into a new situation is sometimes difficult. I would like to make some of these situations easier for all of us!

1. Budgeting is done by department heads. We receive our recommended allocation of funds and work from that figure as a starting point.
2. Leadership roles are "assigned" by you; however, we have always chosen the leaders as a collective group. This seems to make things run smoother in the long run.
3. Hiring of new staff is done as a committee. We include the principal, an assistant principal (of your choice), the department head, and the head of our union.
4. All big decisions are discussed in faculty meetings. We feel as though an open, honest forum for discussing issues is best.

Please know that as a leader of this building, you have my encouragement in this new task that awaits. Feel free to contact me on September 1st, when we begin our contracted school year.

Looking forward to meeting you,

Tom Bradley
President Suburban District Union
Team Leader
Science Teacher

Letter #2

Greetings from your PTO!

We would like to welcome you to Suburban School, home of the Musketeers! We couldn't be happier that you are here with us. We have heard many nice things about you and your potential as a leader.

Please feel free to attend our PTO welcome BBQ at Barney's Pub in Town Square to celebrate your arrival on July 14th. There will be food, drinks, and fun to welcome you to our neighborhood. Please feel free to bring whoever you wish. We want this time to be about YOU!

The Suburban PTO is a rather new organization that is in need of new supporters and helpers. We are always on the lookout for new members that can get involved. We look forward to your involvement and expert leadership.

Thank you for your time and we look forward to a great night at Barney's!

Sincerely,
Joan Betty
PTO President

Letter #3

Dear Principal,

I am writing to welcome you to our community. We need new leadership at Suburban and I'm hoping that your appointment will be as successful as I am hoping.

The minority communities and voices of Suburban need your help. As I have watched my three children grow and move through the grades of Suburban, I have seen a greater and greater disregard for their heritage and cultural identity. There are virtually no programs, clubs, or avenues for our children to grow and be proud of their culture. Our minority students need a principal that will listen to their needs. They need a principal that is willing to stand up to teachers that disrespect and belittle cultural differences. They need a principal that creates opportunities and does not decrease them due to "budgetary constraints." They need a principal that will listen and act.

They need you.

Thank you for taking the time to take in my plea for our students. I anticipate that you will do the right thing for all of us.

Respectfully,
Ashley Robinson

Letter #4

Dear (your first name),

I'm sorry that I couldn't be here on your first big day. I'd like to offer my sincerest congratulations and welcome! I will be on vacation for this entire week in Ocean City, NJ. When I return next Monday, I'd like to meet and get going with what you would like to do for the new school year. I'm ready, willing, and happy to get started. I've been here at Suburban for three years as an assistant principal and want to share some observations (and warn you of a few pitfalls . . . lol). Pencil me in if you can. I know you'll be busy. See you soon,
Jim
James Garrison
Assistant Principal

Letter #5

Dear (your last name):

I'd like to welcome you to your new appointment as principal of Suburban School. You may remember meeting me during the interview process. I was the finalist with you during the last few meetings with the panel. I have been here for seven years and am still one of the current assistant principals of Suburban School. I'd like to congratulate you on a job well done. I know you must be overwhelmed with your new circumstance, which is understandable. Please do not hesitate to contact me for help or other expertise. I look forward to meeting you on my return from my extended vacation to Europe. See you in August.

Pamela Richardson
Assistant Principal
Suburban School

P.S. I worked on the master schedule in May. Do me a favor and have Jim look it over. He's not too busy with summer school. I'll tweak it when I return.

Conclusion

Thank you for your purchase of this text. I hope you have found it to be helpful in your quest to be a principal or your work as a current one. The goal was to give both the theoretical background and the practical applications. Like a quality teacher in-service, the best days are usually the ones where you can bring something back to the classroom. Hopefully, this text has given you a few nuggets to bring back to your school.

In a logical sense, we are what we think. In an emotional one, we are, and everything else depends. The balance between what is and what should be often leads us into the path of conflict. However, in not only accepting conflict but also looking forward to it, we can and will push ourselves and the organization to consistently examine our mission and motives. Remember, the rights of the individual and the rights of the collective are in constant tension in our schools. This force sets the stage for action and balance.

Do not get discouraged by the game. Embrace it! Do not get upset when you cannot get caught up. Smile! Always keep focused on what matters. The students!

You can do this! You already do.

In the words of Dave Matthews, I encourage you to "take these chances."

All the best,
 Tony

Bibliography

Autry, James. *The Servant Leader: How to Build a Creative Team, Develop Great Morale, and Improve Bottom-Line Performance*. New York: Crown Publishing Group, 2004.

Barber, A., and Ulmer, J. *Common Threads: Investigating and Solving School Discipline*. Lanham, MD: Rowman & Littlefield, 2013.

Clabaugh, K. G., and Rozycki, G. E. *Understanding Schools: The Foundations of Education*. New York: Harper & Row, 1990.

Creswell, W. John. *Research Design: Qualitative, Quantitative and Mixed Methods Approaches*, 2nd ed. Thousand Oaks, CA: Sage, 2003.

Fienberg, W., and Soltis, F. J. *School and Society*. New York: Teachers College Press, 1998.

Hall, Edward T. *The Silent Language*. Greenwich, CT: Fawcett, 1959.

Maslow, A. *Motivation and Personality*. New York: Harper, 1954.

O'Donnell Wicklund Pigozzi and Peterson, Architects Inc., VS Furniture, and Bruce Mau Design. *The Third Teacher: 79 Ways You Can Use Design to Transform Teaching and Learning*. New York: Abrams, 2010.

OWP/P Architects, VS Furniture, and Bruce Mau Design. *The Third Teacher: 79 Ways You Can Use Design to Transform Teaching and Learning*. New York: Abrams, 2010.

Tzu, Sun. *The Art of War*. Translated by Lionel Giles. New York: Barnes & Noble, 2012.

About the Author

Anthony Barber, EdD, is the director of teaching and learning in the Springfield School District. He is also an adjunct professor at various universities instructing in graduate and undergraduate education and leadership courses. Dr. Barber is also a coauthor with Jeffrey Ulmer of *Common Threads: Investigating and Solving School Discipline,* a 2013 publication dealing with assisting administrators in handling school discipline issues.